Stress in the Spotlight

Stress in the Spotlight

Managing and Coping with Stress
in the Workplace

Brian Claridge
Freelance Journalist, National Press, UK

and

Cary L. Cooper
*Distinguished Professor of Organizational Psychology
and Health, Lancaster University, UK*

First published 2014 by
PALGRAVE MACMILLAN

Palgrave Macmillan in the UK is an imprint of Macmillan Publishers Limited, registered in England, company number 785998, of Houndmills, Basingstoke, Hampshire RG21 6XS.

Palgrave Macmillan in the US is a division of St Martin's Press LLC, 175 Fifth Avenue, New York, NY 10010.

Palgrave Macmillan is the global academic imprint of the above companies and has companies and representatives throughout the world.

Palgrave® and Macmillan® are registered trademarks in the United States, the United Kingdom, Europe and other countries.

ISBN 978–1–137–29234–6

This book is printed on paper suitable for recycling and made from fully managed and sustained forest sources. Logging, pulping and manufacturing processes are expected to conform to the environmental regulations of the country of origin.

A catalogue record for this book is available from the British Library.

Library of Congress Cataloging-in-Publication Data

Claridge, Brian.
Stress in the spotlight : managing and coping with stress in the workplace / Brian Claridge, Cary L. Cooper.

pages cm

Summary: "Based upon interviews with individuals in high pressure positions, this book provides practical insight about how to identify, tackle and overcome any kind of stress. Interviewees include a bomb disposal expert who neutralized bombs in Afghanistan and Iraq, a leading surgeon at Great Ormond Street Hospital who led a team of specialists to separate twins who were joined at the head, and Kevin Roberts, CEO Worldwide of Saatchi and Saatchi. This inspiring book illustrates how people can overcome obstacles, deal with difficult people, get self-motivated, face challenges, establish goals, avoid work taking over their private life and embrace changes at work"—Provided by publisher.

ISBN 978–1–137–29234–6 (hardback)

1. Job stress. 2. Stress (Psychology) 3. Stress management. I. Cooper, Cary L. II. Title.
HF5548.85.C59 2014
158.7′2—dc23

2014025874

Typeset by MPS Limited, Chennai, India.

Contents

Foreword

By Kelly Hoppen MBE, international interior designer, entrepreneur, and business investor on *Dragons' Den*

All people suffer with stress, there's no question about that! I have never met anyone in business who hasn't encountered stress in one form or another. Facing challenges and overcoming setbacks are par for the course in the highly competitive world of business and this book examines the subject of stress in business in a clear and concise way.

It's aimed at anyone responsible for making important decisions for their companies where the wrong call could have devastating effects. Journalist, Brian Claridge, gives a useful insight into "life at the top" by interviewing people in high-pressure jobs and finds out how they cope with stress; while Professor Cary Cooper offers lots of useful advice and coping strategies on how to deal with stress and make life more enjoyable.

It's a fascinating look at business life and tackles the subject of stress head on. I hope you enjoy the book as much as I did.

www.kellyhoppeninteriors.com

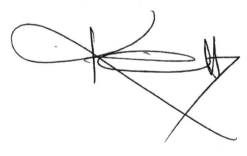

Acknowledgments

This book would not have been possible without the participation of all our interviewees and their invaluable assistance for which we are extremely grateful. Thanks also to Tamsine O'Riordan and the team at Palgrave Macmillan for their excellent support; Gerry Wood at Lancaster University Management School; and to our wives – Denise Claridge and Rachel Cooper, who assisted us throughout the writing of this book. We greatly appreciate all your help and support.

Introduction

From the moment we are born, we are under pressure – to take our first steps, to learn to read and write, to do well at school/college/university, to find a job, to buy a home, and to have a decent burial when we kick the proverbial bucket – the pressures in life are endless!

Are you stressed and unable to cope? Are members of your team showing signs of excessive stress? This book is designed to give you an insight into stress and how others under pressure have coped. It's intended for anyone looking to cope more efficiently in the workplace, whether you're junior, middle, or senior management. We are confident it will make you think more positively about your own pressures, to be more resilient, and to encourage others in your team and organization to be more resilient. You'll get expert advice from people in high-pressure jobs and situations, and be able to find out how they manage to cope with extremely stressful situations in the workplace and achieve the right balance between work and home life, an essential requirement for anyone in business.

This is not a self-help book (there are enough of them already). Instead, we give you a fascinating insight into "life at the top" by carrying out interviews with successful businessmen and women, and others in high pressure jobs, who have managed to achieve success despite setbacks and other obstacles – everyone has different ways of tackling stress in the workplace. You'll be able to find out about various coping strategies, and how our high profile interviewees got to where they are today.

Identifying stress and its costs

Stress has found as firm a place in our modern lexicon as iPads, social media, and junk food. We use the term casually to describe a wide range of symptoms resulting from our hectic pace of life. "I feel stressed," someone says to describe a vague yet often acute sense of distress. "He's under a lot of stress," we say when trying to understand a colleague's irritability. "It's a high-stress job," someone else will say, awarding an odd sort of prestige to his or her occupation. But to those whose ability to cope with day-to-day matters is at crisis point, the concept of stress is no longer a casual one. Pressure is stimulating and motivating, but when pressure exceeds your ability to cope, you are in the stress zone.

Stress and the consequent mental ill health affects nearly one in four of the working population, and over the years has become the leading cause of sickness absence in the workplace. The Centre for Mental Health has estimated the direct costs of sickness absence, presenteeism (going to work ill and contributing little value to the service or product) and labor turnover was £26b per annum. In addition, stress and mental ill health represent roughly 40% of all incapacity benefit in the UK, at nearly £5b a year.

Stress comes in a variety of forms, from behavioral symptoms to physical symptoms to ill health outcomes (not only mental ill health, but also as a risk factor in a range of physical conditions). When the pressure exceeds the individual's ability to cope, the first symptoms are behavioral (e.g. losing your sense of humor, constant irritability with people, constant tiredness, suppressed anger, difficulty making decisions, difficulty concentrating). The next phase is where the individual displays physical symptoms (e.g. insomnia, lack of appetite or excessive craving for food, headaches, nausea, frequent indigestion or heartburn, non-specific aches and pains). And finally, if the original underlying sources of the stress persist, and an individual's coping strategies aren't working effectively, they can turn into risk factors for a range of illnesses (e.g. depression/ anxiety, heart disease, chronic fatigue syndrome, immune system disorders).

This book will show you ways of dealing with stress quickly and effectively in order to prevent it leading to mental health issues and a possible breakdown, by drawing on the experiences of people in stressful jobs who have (or have had) to cope with enormous pressure. They include a bomb disposal expert in his ceaseless battle against terrorism in some of the most dangerous places on earth, and a surgeon who performed a ground-breaking operation with a specialist team to separate twins who were joined at the head.

Most of the interviewees are successful businessmen and women, including Dame Mary Perkins, who with her husband Doug founded the highly successful company Specsavers, which secured them a place in the *Sunday Times* Rich List. Other high-profile subjects in the book include Frederick Forsyth, international bestselling author; Chris Bonington, world-famous mountaineer, explorer, and writer; Jeff Banks, international fashion designer; and Ken Hom, international celebrity chef, author, and television presenter. Discover how they achieved international success and overcame stress and setbacks. Here are a few quotes from some of our high-profile interviewees – read their full interviews in the book.

> Focus, commitment, and discipline are at the heart of my stress management program, and if you rigorously, relentlessly, and joyfully implement these, you never lose the ability to cope. Stress, worry, regret, pain, and guilt are all emotions that must be managed, reduced, or eliminated and replaced with positive behaviors.
>
> **Kevin Roberts,**
> **CEO Worldwide, Saatchi & Saatchi**

> Stress is part of life! The key is to act promptly to avoid a build-up. My strategies for dealing with stress: (1) Exercise each morning – it clears the mind; (2) Discuss any issues with personal and business partners – they include my wife, business partner, lawyer, accountant, and clients; and (3) Deal with issues promptly and work to avoid build-up.
>
> **Gale D. Metzger,**
> **Former Co-Founder & President of Statistical Research, Inc.**

> In the surreal high-stakes, high-pressure world I was living in, where every decision could have been my last, I grew to learn that fear can be

your friend. Confucius once said: "Our greatest glory is not in never failing, but in rising each time we fail." He was bang-on. Instead of allowing fear to curtail success, you can use it to give you an edge. Visualizing a successful outcome and learning breathing-techniques also helped!

Major Chris Hunter,
Former bomb disposal expert, author, and broadcaster

The author team consists of journalist Brian Claridge, who came up with the idea for the book and conducted the interviews, and psychologist Cary Cooper, who provides expert analyses to explain the lessons to be learnt in each case, as well as giving expert advice on some of the best ways of coping with stress in the workplace.

Here are just a few of the valuable management tips in the book, which are highlighted in the Conclusion section:

- Be flexible. In order to cope with all the stresses and strains of pressured jobs, we need to adapt to everything that is thrown at us in the workplace and in life. We need to get away from a rigid mentality and behavioral set, epitomized by this humorous quote from Samuel Goldwyn "I'm willing to admit that I may not always be right, but I am never wrong."
- Share your concerns with someone you trust, whether a partner/spouse, close friend, or family member. Keeping problems repressed is an unhealthy coping strategy. This is closely allied to seeking social support if you need it, rather than trying to be a macho man/woman. It is all too easy in business to hide your problems behind a veneer of self-confidence, a problem which in the end can eat away at you and cause serious health problems.
- Never look back and say "I wish I had" or "I should have." Learn from your mistakes but don't dwell on them. The people who get ahead in life are those that have a "bounce-back" mentality. They say "I have failed, I will learn from this," and then get on with the next venture without wallowing in the failure.

Learn from "real life experience" how to:

- Cope with the pressures of the workplace.
- Overcome obstacles.

- Deal with difficult people in the workplace.
- Get self-motivated.
- Face life's challenges.
- Establish a goal.
- Cope with failure.
- Avoid work taking over your private life.
- Embrace changes at work, rather than fight them.

chapter 1

Kevin Roberts – CEO Worldwide, Saatchi & Saatchi

Kevin Roberts is the New York-based CEO Worldwide of Saatchi & Saatchi, one of the world's leading creative organizations, with over 6000 people and 130 offices in 70 countries.

Born and educated in Lancaster in the north of England, Kevin started his career in the late 1960s with iconic London fashion house Mary Quant. He became a senior marketing executive for Gillette and Procter & Gamble in Europe and the Middle East. At 32 he became CEO of Pepsi-Cola Middle East, and later Pepsi's CEO in Canada. In 1989, Kevin moved with his family to Auckland, New Zealand, to become Chief Operating Officer with Lion Nathan. He took up his position as CEO Worldwide with Saatchi & Saatchi in 1997.

Kevin is Honorary Professor of Creative Leadership at Lancaster University and Honorary Professor of Innovation and Creativity at the University of Auckland Business School. He is the author or co-author of Peak Performance *and* Lovemarks *and further books on the power of emotion and the screen age.* Lovemarks *was named one of the ten Ideas of the Decade by Advertising Age in 2009.*

In 2013 Kevin, a New Zealand citizen, was made a Companion of the New Zealand Order of Merit (CNZM) for services to business and the community. A former director of the New Zealand Rugby Union, he is the current Chairman of the Board of USA Rugby, a Director of New Zealand Telecom, and business ambassador for the New Zealand United States Council.

About Kevin

"I am the CEO Worldwide for global advertising agency, Saatchi & Saatchi. I like ideas and inspiration and hate the word 'but'. I am the originator of Lovemark thinking, the methodology that differentiates Saatchi & Saatchi from all our competitors.

I was born in a council house in Bowerham, Lancaster. My parents were working class, with very little education. My father was a security guard in a mental hospital (not unlike my current job in many ways!), and my mother managed a small shop selling greeting cards. I went to the local primary school. As a young child, I was left with my grandma every day while my parents were at work. My grandma cleaned people's houses and we developed a terrific relationship which I sustained through my teens until she died.

My father loved sport and encouraged me to play soccer and cricket. He had left school at 14 and was part of a large family of seven brothers and sisters. My mother had one other sister who had successfully passed the 11+ and gone to Lancaster Girls' Grammar School. My Auntie Enyd was my supporter, mentor, and great believer in the power of education as the foundation for progress.

My parents were rather negative and socialists. As far as they were concerned, my brother, sister, and I were all destined to continue in the working class, to leave school early, to get a job, and to not leave the environment from which we came. We were pretty strapped growing up, with very little money for luxuries. My parents both smoked heavily, which is where a lot of the disposable money went. I have often told people that I have been poor and I have been rich, and being rich is better. I found little nobility in poverty as I felt that influence and impact were limited by those with more money, power, and clout than us.

There is no question that as a 14-year-old my greatest motivator was the Animals song, "'We gotta get out of this place – if it's the last thing we ever do." I was lucky enough to pass the 11+ and go to Lancaster Royal Grammar School, which motivated me immensely. I was a high achiever in rugby, athletics, and cricket, and was also in the Alpha stream academically. I was surrounded by ambitious, bright, hard-working kids who inspired me to do the same. I was lucky enough to be made captain of many of the teams I played for and this gave me the responsibility on which I've thrived.

I had started captaining the football and cricket teams at Bowerham when I was 9 or 10 and have enjoyed leadership roles ever since. The most significant thing that has ever occurred to me was being expelled from LRGS as a Sixth Former, having been asked by the school to captain the First XI the next year and likely captaining the First XV too.

My first girlfriend, Barbara Beckett, became pregnant largely because no one had told me anything about birth control, either at home or at school. It happened the second time we did it! The headmaster of LRGS took a dim view of this and said I could not stay at school and have the baby. I was very much in love with Barbara and with my working class background we did not desert girls in need. So instead of a university career and who knows what ahead of me, overnight I was married with a baby, no money, no savings, no prospects – and no clue as to what I would do. The biggest business in town was Storeys of Lancaster and I rocked up there as a 17-year-old with a good working knowledge of French and Spanish (which was something of a rarity in Lancaster in those days). I was put to work immediately in the export operation, where my linguistic skills compensated for my lack of experience, and my cricket skills were much in demand by the office manager, Tommy Blacow, who was part of the hiring process. He took me down to his cricket team, Heysham, to play. So I landed (accidentally) in Sales and Marketing, which I loved from the start and never left."

What makes a successful business person?

"To reach the top you must be a radical optimist who is purpose driven. I believe that the role of business is to make the world a better place for everyone, which allows me to be a passionate advocate for business itself. Inspirational leadership is critical. By that I mean that today's leaders are not the command and control type, nor indeed servant leaders. Instead they focus on inspiring everyone they touch to be the best they can be in pursuit of the company's dream. Successful leaders today are ideas driven and know how to create a culture where ideas flourish.

At the heart of business success is the ability to eradicate guilt, regret, and fear and replace these powerful emotions with ambition, belief, and passion. Leaders today must embrace Vince Lombardi's maxim, 'Winning isn't everything but wanting to win is,' because business is, and will ever remain, a blood sport.

Tom Peters got it right: fail fast, learn fast, fix fast. With the emphasis on the latter two, and on the fast. Setbacks are a way of life in business and happen on a daily basis. The New Zealand rugby team, the All Blacks, fear failure more than they revere success and this fear of failure keeps them focused. I make 30 decisions a day and ten of them are wrong. The trick is to follow the Tom Peters' maxim, to spend very little time navel gazing and to focus on the killer app, which is execution. Success does not come from getting things done, it comes from making things happen. The best way to bounce back from a problem is to make something happen quickly.

The best business investment I made was in Saatchi & Saatchi stock, which was at £1.13 per share when I joined the company. Two years later, when I sold the company to Publicis, we secured a price of £5 per share. My worst business investment is yet to come.

Decision-making is based on information and knowledge primarily. From there you add insight (or rather revelations) and foresight. A combination of these four reduces risk, but fundamentally the ideas business is a very risky environment because an idea is only an idea once, which means it has never been seen before and it isn't possible to fully mitigate this kind of risk.

I believe in making the big decisions with the heart, and the little ones with my head. At my age, there is very little that could happen to me that hasn't already happened in a business sense, so I rely on my experience, judgment, and intuition. Interrogating the data usually results in everyone coming up with the same answers. Winning comes from finding an answer that no one else has thought of.

My biggest company successes include:

- Pepsi-Cola going past Coca-Cola in Canada.
- Lion Nathan becoming the largest brewer in Australia.
- Saatchi & Saatchi becoming Agency of the Year globally a few years back.

I'm not careful and I have no concept of overspending. I avoid care and moderation whenever possible. Nothing succeeds like excess and in many cases I go into projects with a 'sky's the limit' budget and still manage to overspend. People inevitably forget how much it costs or how long it took when they see how beautiful it is and how effective it is. Risk limitation and minimization as a going-in position is a very limiting mindset.

I never patent and protect my business ideas. Lovemarks, which is one of the bigger marketing ideas, was never patented. My board told me to and I disagreed and refused. I told them ideas were open source and it was a question of 'use them or lose them.'

Partnerships are important but leadership is more important. Leaders are the deciders (George Bush got a lot of things wrong but he was right on this). Shimon Peres told me that leadership is a very lonely place and that leaders must have the courage to be afraid.

So whilst companies operate more effectively with collaboration and partnership, leaders inevitably face many moments of loneliness, which they must welcome. As the Cadillac ad said in the early 1900s, this is the penalty of leadership.

Growth is the name of the game. For inclusive capitalism to work, it must deliver growth. It must deliver jobs, opportunities, and ways for individuals to develop higher self-esteem. Most people do this through achievement and winning. Mankind is fundamentally competitive and wants to improve.

Timing, frankly, is what you make it and is driven by pure, stupid luck, or serendipity. My only thought on this is to suck it and see. Get lots of little ideas out there fast all the time. In today's world, circumstances and consumers change so quickly that planning and predicting is self-indulgent. Get it out there, test it, and see what happens."

How do you deal with stress?

"I prioritize everything daily and as part of that prioritization I keep 50% of my time every day free to deal with the unexpected. Inevitably, it is the unexpected that becomes the game-breaker. Filling one's days with the business of doing business is a futile and unrewarding exercise. In a VUCA (Volatile, Uncertain, Complex, Ambiguous) world, it's impossible to predict what's coming at you. The trick is to ensure you have the mental energy, the heart, and the time to deal with the unexpected. It is the important that matters, not the urgent.

As Woody Allen said, 'Relationships are like sharks, once they stop moving they die.' The same thing applies to business. Toyota taught me this. There is always a better way and I'm keen to try it and find it. I spend little time assessing and deciding. I put my focus on executing and refining.

If I can't resolve a problem, I head for the spaces where I'm most creative, such as my house in Grasmere, and I think about something completely different. My reptilian brain kicks in, my intuition is free to operate, and 12 hours later a new approach always presents itself. I never share the problem with anyone else and I don't solve problems in groups or by talking about them.

I was lucky enough to spend a couple of hours with President Shimon Peres in Tel Aviv talking about leadership last year. One of the things he told me was 'What is controversial today is inevitably popular tomorrow.' Negative reaction to my ideas, therefore, is like water off a duck's back. I was once told that to run Saatchi & Saatchi effectively you need to every morning 'strap on a waterproof back and a bulletproof vest.' I do, every day.

I never switch off from work mode, because I don't have a work mode. I have only one mode, which is to be the best I can be in everything I do. I'm a believer in the Oprah Winfrey quote 'Live your best life every day.' So for me work/life balance is a crock. Balance is to be avoided at all costs. I believe in work/life integration. I want to be the best at business, sport, friendship, parenting, family as I can be. And I want to be happy in every moment I have. You are responsible for your own happiness and my happiness comes from doing things I love and inspiring people I touch.

Technology today has liberated us so I can be just as effective away from the office as I can be in the office. And I make maximum use of this.

I subscribe to the view that 'Living well is the best revenge,' and having been born poor I really appreciate the finer things of life. I have, however, rarely been in debt. I am determined that no one will ever take me back to where I came and, therefore, didn't buy my first house until I was 39. I bought it for cash. I now own a bunch of properties that I live in different parts of the world, all of which I paid for in cash. I collect art, again, all of which I pay for in cash. I don't trade or sell art. I buy it to keep and give away to my family and friends. I never, ever gamble. Life is too tough to throw money away. I've always backed myself to earn more than I spend. And so far I'm just about ahead (if only fractionally!).

Stress is something you have to actively recognize and work on. I've always been behind the '8' ball, having no tertiary education and no network to rely on so, frankly, working harder has always been my killer app. I've been determined to enjoy a life well lived, which also brings its own share of stress. In my experience, you have to recognize this and first know thyself. Figure out what stresses you out and either eliminate it from your life, or reduce it massively, and replace it with things you enjoy, which minimize the stress. This needs to be very specific. Stress, worry, regret, pain, and guilt are all emotions that must be managed, reduced, or eliminated and replaced with positive behavior.

Focus, commitment and discipline are at the heart of my stress management program and if you rigorously, relentlessly, and joyfully implement these, you never lose the ability to cope.

There are no work situations now that cause me stress. Stress for me comes from family situations such as illness, relationships, etc. that I cannot totally control. When faced with these inevitable situations, I try to remain calm, quiet, and empathetic whilst quickly moving to implementing some kind of action. In any crisis I have found calmness and purposeful commitment to action is what is required and appreciated.

My advice to people who find it difficult to cope with stress at work or home: change your job. Find something you are passionate about that doesn't cause stress.

We look for employees who are competitive, passionate, restless team players driven by ideas. We look for collaborators and connectors who are purpose driven and who get on well with others. We believe in giving them responsibility, learning, recognition, and joy. This generally results in them being happy and as we know, happy bunnies work more productively than unhappy bunnies.

I'm accessible to everyone and answer all emails personally within 24 hours. And I mean all of them. And I mean personally.

I also run many KR Live and KR Unplugged sessions for talent around the network of all ages.

I hate firing people. It is my biggest weakness. I would have made a terrible rugby coach as I would never have been able to drop loyal, older players. Even now it takes me 12 months to do what others could do in three months. I always do it personally.

I always ensure people who leave, leave with their dignity and integrity intact. And I'm convinced that many of them are more successful elsewhere. It is usually not a reflection of their ability, but more of their attitude or fit that prevents them being the best they can be at Saatchi & Saatchi. I take the greatest pleasure in seeing them succeed elsewhere.

Humor is vital. Responsibility, learning, recognition, are nothing without joy. Depressed employees are non-productive. Happy employees make the company a better place. Work with people you like. Do something you love. And make things happen.

Would I do things the same way if I started from scratch? Bob Seelert, Saatchi & Saatchi Chairman, once told me: 'Start with the answer and work back.' Priceless advice."

ANALYSIS AND ADVICE

There are a number of generic points we can learn from this interview. First, that deprivation and failure can be the precursors for success. It has been found in numerous studies (see Cooper & Hingley, *The Change Makers*; Cox & Cooper, *High Flyers*) that experiencing loss or deprivation can motivate individuals to achieve, to gain control of a world later in life that they were unable to control when they were younger.

Second, many successful people in a variety of walks of life have experienced profound life events early that were the drivers of their success later in life. These adverse life events can lead to the development of effective coping strategies. One significant one is "to take control" rather than relinquish it. A great deal of psychological research has found that those people who have an "internal locus of control," who don't let external events control them, but take control and look for options to deal with problems, are the ones who cope better and have fewest negative outcomes.

Third, the fear of failure can also be a good motivator, enabling the individual to learn new and more resilient coping strategies. As Henry Ford once said "failure is only the opportunity to begin again more intelligently."

Fourth, different coping strategies are appropriate for different situations, and one size does not fit all stressful situations. As Mark Twain once wrote "if you always do what you always did, you'll always get what you always got."

chapter 2

Dame Mary Perkins DBE – Co-Founder and Senior Executive, Specsavers

Dame Mary founded Specsavers in 1984 with husband Doug and has since grown the business to become the largest, privately owned optical company in the world.

Born in Bristol, Dame Mary qualified as an optometrist after attending Cardiff University, where she met Doug. Together they bought out Mary's father's optical business when he retired and gradually built up their family-friendly opticians in the West Country and Wales, selling up and moving to Guernsey in 1981 where the joint venture concept of Specsavers was born.

Dame Mary was honored by the Queen for her services to business and the community in 2007. The same year, she was named the most outstanding woman in business at the National Business Awards. She was also the first recipient of the First Women Lifetime Achievement award, in 2010.

She supports numerous charities and is patron of everywoman and anti-bullying charity Kidscape, an ambassador for Vision Aid Overseas, Sightsavers, and Action Aid, a Liveryman of the Worshipful Company of Spectacle Makers and Freeman of the City of London. She is also an Honorary Chartered Director of the Institute of Directors, an Honorary Fellow of Cardiff University and she has been awarded an Honorary Doctorate from Plymouth University.

About Mary

"I was born in the center of Bristol in 1944 and lived with my grandparents who were both tailors. I moved to the outskirts of Bristol to live in a prefab with the joy of an inside toilet and proper bathroom a little late and in 1955 I passed the 11+ to go to Fairfield Grammar School. My father worked in a cotton mill, as did much of his family. He left his birthplace of Wallasey to come to Bristol in the 30s, where his sister was 'in service', and became errand boy for a chemist. When the NHS started in 1948/49, there was a 'fast course' to become optometrists, as the free NHS glasses were in such demand, which he did by going to night school three nights a week. After he qualified he worked for himself and gradually grew the business I was to work in during the school holidays, as I made up my mind to become an optometrist. I took A level sciences at school, very unusual for girls then. I would have loved to have done English and History, but needed to get to Cardiff Advanced Technology College to do the three-year Optics and Visual Science course plus one year after before taking professional exams.

My father always believed in affordable glasses for everyone – and his prices were very affordable – everyone on our council estate came to him, and he offered two for the price of one! So I became an optometrist because of my father, and his ethos of affordable and complete prices and his ideas of 2–4–1 and 'Kids go Free' passed on to me.

We never had money to spare when I was growing up – I made all my own clothes and we didn't have holidays, except for a short break self-catering in Weymouth – however, as young people we never 'wanted things'." I went to the Church Youth Club, Girl Guides, church outings, and played in the streets or went for walks in the countryside.

As a student I was always hard up and once working, my husband and I had to be careful. We saved hard for a deposit on a house and managed with curtains and some furniture from relatives.

I went straight into my own business with my husband, as qualified optometrist, but having to do all sorts of other things – accounts, purchasing, hiring staff, training, etc.

As the business grew, naturally, it was easier. But it was our own business – if we didn't work, then no money came in. I took ten days off to have my children and worked right up to having them, six days a week *plus* three evenings to 9:00 p.m. But my motivation was to have a successful business – this was pre Specsavers. The original optical business was sold in 1980 for £2 million.

It was always planned that Specsavers would become national, covering one region at a time (aided by TV advertising), but we thought that would mean about 200 stores. We were ambitious, but it was impossible to look too far ahead. Our most challenging decision was to 'break ranks' and advertise clearly to the customer what prices were and what offers were available – not done before Specsavers started, although Margaret Thatcher had just 'de-regulated' professions, which allowed for more openness.

The main decision (although an easy one) was not to own the stores but to run them on a joint venture partnership with a local resident optometrist director working 40 hours/week in the store, and having the profits of the store. We would just be paid for the support services we did.

We currently have Specsavers in ten countries – UK, Republic of Ireland, Norway, Sweden, Finland, Denmark, Netherlands, Spain, NZ and Australia. We still have a great deal to do in the countries we are trading in now, plus an expansion with our hearing services (we currently have tenders to carry out NHS work in the UK).

Specsavers statistics:

30,000 + employees
2000 + partners
12 million frames sold
290 million + contact lenses sold
240,000 hearing tests conducted
1659 stores.

The press claims of me being the sixth richest woman in UK are pure speculation. I believe they based the figure on whatever the company is worth – but I have no idea how anyone (other than myself and my husband) would know any details, as we are a private company in Guernsey, and we don't own the stores. Accounts for stores and other trading in UK (e.g. manufacturing, etc.) are published in Companies House and UK tax paid on all profits in the UK (other countries are the same). I certainly have no money worries as such and I still work full-time. I get paid a management fee for services done and for the Brand – we have about 550 people employed at our offices in Guernsey and we are the largest commercial employer.

We carry out undercover disguises from time to time to see how the stores are doing. It is true I did this in the past, but having spoken at many of our seminars and met so many staff, they would recognize me now. Plus our customer service is at the heart of everything we do, with a lot of training, so I rest easier and don't go into stores in disguise – but I do still visit many of them. We have many initiatives in place to learn quickly from our customers what they feel and a great team of Retail Development Managers who visit the stores and who can help where needed."

How do you cope with stress?

"I was highly honored to be named Dame Commander for services to business and to the community in Guernsey. Finding time to do all the various duties requires dedication to the job.

I keep a diary of everything and I am prepared to work anytime – that means 24/7 if needs be. I am starting to get a bit stricter now and am learning to say 'no', but I do enjoy the mixture of things and also we encourage all staff, in support offices and in stores, to do volunteering and charity work. (A big award each year to see which store has done the most in their community.)

My three children work for the business; however, they don't live at home – two are married and have children themselves. It's impossible to keep work and home life separate. We find it's best if we have the grandchildren at family gatherings so we don't talk business as much!

At home, Doug and I have separate studies so we can have peace and quiet, albeit on our own! We both like keeping fit (yoga, Qi Gong, walking) and Guernsey is a lovely place to relax in. Doug follows rugby and I sing in a choir, so we have other topics than work to talk about!

Our aim for the future is to continue to be Number 1 in whatever market we are in and to keep to Our Vision and Values and Our Partnerships.

The six key points in being successful in whatever field you work in are:

- Keep to the vision and values (no 'spray').
- Develop staff to be the best they can be/good succession people planning.
- Be a good leader, setting clear goals.
- Be close to your customers.
- Work hard at innovation and differentiation.
- Use your common sense and gut feeling (don't get carried away with 'outside' advice).

When you are No. 1, act as No. 2 and never become complacent.

Both Doug and I have learnt from successes and failures – luckily more successes than failures.

Fortunately, we have never had any setbacks in business. In terms of organization, I like to finish my day with a list of what I want to do the next day – if I'm away a lot in the week then I will use the weekend to catch up on emails, letters, board meeting notes, etc. – all ready for my PA of long-standing (and long-suffering) to do on a Monday morning.

If something unexpected comes along, then I just do it, and the other stuff waits or gets done when possible even if that is much later in the day/evening. I don't have a whole department of staff to lead, so in a way, my life is easier and freer to chop and change my day.

If I'm stuck in a rut and can't resolve a problem, I bounce if off my husband! He does the same to me – frequently. If he wasn't there, then it would be a brainstorming session, or I'll shut myself away to work on the problem. I wouldn't sleep on it, because it would keep me awake (I sleep with pen and paper by my bedside as it is).

Brainstorming, done properly, is great – our Green Blood people can solve many problems that I am not able to. I am a great believer in teamwork as I believe in doing something right first time, which means the more there are working on a problem or project, the better the outcome.

However, there must be an accountability within the team – no procrastinators, or sitting on the fence. I like teams, cross-functional if possible, to do things other than work – e.g. volunteering in their community (paint a hall, dig a garden, etc.).

My work never affects my mood. I'm luckier than most in so far that my husband is the 'release valve'. I now have the most amazing, dependable people all across the business that I can rely on completely. I get upset personally if a customer doesn't get exceptional service, as I want everything to be perfect – I'm a bit of a perfectionist.

My strategy for relaxing is:

- listening to music and singing.
- yoga.
- a good myotherapy massage.
- Qi Gong session (similar to Tai Chi – think of those Chinese early in the morning in the park doing movements).

If you suffer with stress or have a work-related problem, the best thing to do is to talk about it either to a work colleague, or to HR if you work for a large company. Work out why the stress is there in the first place, write the problem down and it will hopefully resolve itself once you've worked out the root cause.

Stress at home – there are many reasons for this, which can't be easily resolved. Things like job insecurity, lack of money, teenage problems, and long hours at work. It helps to talk and to share the anxieties with someone you know well. Health is all-important, so make sure you eat healthily, get plenty of exercise and fresh air, and a good night's sleep. Learn some relaxation techniques and take time out (not necessarily off work) and have some quality 'me' time.

The qualities I look for from my employees are that they must be 'techni-cally' fit for the job. After that it's their general manner and willingness to learn and progress. They will have goals to work toward (done at appraisals) and, subject to their performance, they will be able to enjoy a profit share, as well as quarterly performance bonuses.

I am always accessible (as are the main board) to employees at our open plan office in Guernsey. Each of our stores is an individual limited company owned by the local resident optician(s) and myself/husband in Guernsey on a joint venture partnership. The optician(s) are responsible for the day-to-day running of their store and their staff. I meet all the managers at the regional and national seminars, and many visit our support offices in Guernsey, Southampton, and Nottingham. I also visit Southampton and Nottingham to meet the support staff and many of them often come to Guernsey (a daily company plane flies them to Guernsey). Communication is key in the whole Specsavers' business, and we meet the 2000 partners every eight weeks for a day to discuss just about anything – it's two-way communication.

I use humor sometimes when a meeting is tackling a tricky issue. It doesn't help to be full of doom and gloom when you are trying to resolve a problem, especially as we are all striving to get a good result.

My advice for dealing with the pressure of entrepreneurship is:

- Involve your family as you will be completely absorbed in your business (I always involved my children).
- Don't over stretch or spread yourself too thinly in trying to do too many things.
- Stick to what you know and know your market/customers inside out.
- Don't be pushed in a wrong direction by investors (they always want you to expand and give them a good fast return – they don't often have your long-term vision).
- You don't have to be big in lots of countries to be successful.
- Differentiate from others in your field.
- Build a brand.

The most important lessons I have learnt about business are:

- To know when 'phase 1' is coming to an end and when it's time to bring 'specialists' into the board.
- To know when the business has outgrown the skills of people who may have been with you since the beginning (and are now your friends!).
- Do your own research thoroughly – I do not rely on reports from others.
- Have a passion for the work you do. If you view it as a chore – get out!

I enjoy going to work each day – we work hard and play hard as well. What on earth would I do all day if I didn't work? There's always charity work, but a lot of that is linked to work.

Each day is different plus I get to travel around as well – and people are very nice to me!"

ANALYSIS AND ADVICE

There are a number of insights that come from this interview that will help us all understand high-pressure jobs and how to deal with them. First, the issue of the importance of taking risks comes up – not only from the point of view of being successful in a job, but also that by creating the Big Hairy Audacious Goals in life, you stretch yourself and learn to cope with the challenges these risks create. Sir James Goldsmith once wrote "the ultimate risk is not taking risk," or as Winston Churchill said "To improve is to change, to be perfect is to change often."

Second, to cope with all the stresses and strains of pressured jobs, we need to be flexible. We all need to adapt to everything that is thrown at us in the workplace and in life more generally ... we need to get away from a rigid mentality and behavioral set, epitomized by this humorous quote from Samuel Goldwyn "I'm willing to admit that I may not always be right, but I am never wrong."

Third, we also need some space to reflect on those things that trouble us, some "peaceful space" to reflect on how we should deal with an issue rather than just reacting emotionally immediately.

Fourth is about sharing your concerns with someone you trust, whether a partner/spouse, close friend or family member. Keeping problems repressed is an unhealthy coping strategy. This is closely allied to seeking "social support" if you need it, rather than trying to be macho man/woman. It is all too easy in business to hide your problems behind a veneer of self-confidence, a problem which in the end can eat away at you and cause serious health problems.

And finally, do those everyday things that make you relax and unwind for a short time: what we call "recovery activities," such as swimming, listening to music, relaxation exercises, or taking a walk. Churchill found solace during the war in painting, as a way of taking time out from the multiple demands and long hours.

chapter 3

Major Chris Hunter QGM – Former Bomb Disposal Expert, Author, and Broadcaster

Since retiring from the army, Major Chris Hunter has worked as a counter-terrorism consultant, writer, and broadcaster. He is a Fellow of the Institute of Explosives Engineers, a Member of the International Association of Bomb Technicians and Investigators and a regular contributor to television and radio news and current affairs programs.

He rounded off his military career as the senior intelligence analyst for world-wide IED activity at the Ministry of Defence. At the time of the London suicide bombings, he was seconded to Cobra, the Cabinet Office's emergency response committee.

Major Hunter has written about his former role as a bomb-disposal expert in Extreme Risk – A Life Fighting the Bombmakers. *For his actions during his Iraq tour, he was awarded the Queen's Gallantry Medal by HM Queen Elizabeth II.*

About Chris

"I was born in my parent's pub in Hertfordshire. My earliest memories are of constantly meeting a seemingly endless flow of fascinating adults in the bar; being bullied and looked after by my three older brothers – in equal measure – and of spending quality time with my parents on their rare days off. I vividly remember, as a young child, watching *Danger UXB* with my father, who was a WWII bomb disposal officer; and in particular seeing the torment and pressure on his face; his hands would shake; his breathing would become shallow and fast; he'd drift into another world, another life … his former life. We'd be watching it together, only he wouldn't just be watching it; he'd be re-living it.

My parents weren't wealthy, but they were definitely entrepreneurial. They'd take on pubs that weren't particularly successful then turn them around. They were very good at it. When my parents split up, my father retired and my mother re-married and for two or three years we certainly struggled financially; that all changed when my mum and stepfather bought a restaurant in Hay-on-Wye. It was a success from day one, but those intervening lean years taught me a valuable lesson in life. There are many people out there who know the cost of everything and the value of nothing. As for my motivation for being successful, it was simple: I have never competed against anybody in my life, but always pushed myself to the limit. I was a keen sportsman, but in particular I loved cross-country running. If I came first I took it in my stride; but equally, if I was beaten it never bothered me … as long as I knew I'd given it my best shot. It's a lesson that became very much a foundation of my personality.

My father died when I was 15 and I very much went off the rails. As a result I wasn't particularly academic at school, but thankfully I did have an above average IQ. So when I joined the Army at 16, I was selected to train as a Russian linguist – working in military intelligence. It was tough academically, but the rigid military structure in which we studied helped a great deal, and crucially it inspired me to have a thirst for knowledge, which thankfully has continued throughout my working life.

One of my brothers, my father, grandfather, and great-grandfather were all military men at various points in their lives, so I guess you could say it was in my genes; but the real career-shaping moment for me was after one of my brothers killed himself. He had been dealt a poor hand in life and eventually ended up as a drug dealer, with a severe disability and acute depression. After his death – and while I was at Sandhurst training to become an officer – I seriously reconsidered my future in the Army and for a brief time considered working in counter-narcotics. My company commander told me that if I wanted to have a genuine and tangible effect on countering narcotics, the best thing I could do is work in counter-terrorism. He suggested I train as a Counter-Terrorist Bomb Disposal Operator and from that moment the seed was firmly planted.

I began life as a Russian linguist working in military intelligence, but to be honest, while I could do the job adequately I was never that great at it. By the time I was 19 I was identified as being 'officer material', and after a short spell working as a leadership trainer I went to Sandhurst and it was while I was there that I initially embraced the idea of becoming a bomb disposal operator.

Shortly after finishing my officer training at Sandhurst, I was deployed to Bosnia, where I witnessed some terrible atrocities including genocide and ethnic cleansing. As a result, I briefly considered doing something other than training as a bomb disposal operator – perhaps attempting selection for the special forces; but that all changed on my next tour when I was working as a troop commander in Northern Ireland. While I was driving into the British Army's headquarters there, I witnessed two IRA car bombs explode in a packed car park inside the barracks. It was rush hour, so as you can imagine, the first bomb caused numerous injuries; the second exploded a few minutes later, this time outside the medical center. It had been placed there deliberately to target the wounded. I was so sickened by the callousness of the attacks, but hugely inspired by the bravery of the bomb disposal operators who searched the remaining hundreds of parked cars by hand while those at risk were busy being evacuated. That was the moment I decided for sure I was going to be a bomb technician. That moment was my calling.

My former job as a bomb disposal expert has been described as the most dangerous job on the planet. What made me do it? I know some do it for the adrenalin rush, others to seek atonement for darker episodes in their lives. But I think most do it out of a good old-fashioned sense of duty – just because they want to make a difference. For me, I guess it's a bit of all three.

I suppose the real question is, what makes us stay? There's something immensely gratifying about neutralizing a weapon designed to kill and maim large numbers of people. Everybody I know who does it is absolutely hooked. It has to be one of the most interesting jobs on the planet. It didn't just challenge and motivate me mentally; the fact that we got to save the lives of thousands of people we didn't know and would more than likely never meet was massively inspiring on a spiritual level too. Not a single day goes by now when somebody isn't killed by an IED.

But I guess if I put my hand on my heart, the biggest, most powerful incentive was the buzz. Rendering safe a terrorist bomb is probably the most exciting thing I've ever done without getting arrested. The rush I got from dealing with a device was fearsome. It's living on the edge. It's truly elemental; a world where everything is black and white; a world of straightforward choices. Life and death. It comes at a cost, of course. One minute you're standing at the cliff's edge, just you and the bomb, pushing it to the max; the next you're at home with your wife and kids, trying to calm down and be normal again. And if you're living on the edge, eventually you're going to go all the way over. If you're lucky, you see the signs and decide it's time to pull back and step away.

The grueling regime at Sandhurst when I was a young officer helped to prepare me for the tough and dangerous work that lay ahead. I spent the majority of my time at Sandhurst cold, wet, tired, and miserable. Soldiering is often dirty, unpleasant, and brutal work, and training exercises – necessarily – are no exception. It's impossible to entirely replicate the stresses of combat, but the grueling regime at Sandhurst is about as close as it gets in peacetime. And the leadership training there is second to none. That said, the aim of Sandhurst is only to prepare young men and women to lead soldiers in combat. An officer's training continues throughout his or her career. One of the best pieces of leadership advice was given to me by my first Troop Sergeant in Bosnia. He said: 'Never have a wishbone where your backbone should be, and always follow the three Rs: respect for yourself, respect for others and responsibility for your actions.'

The closest I've come to losing my life on the battlefield was on 8 May 2004. We'd neutralized three bombs in Basrah, Iraq, that day and had been out on the ground for over 16 hours without a break. Just as we were passing through the city, looking forward to climbing into our beds, my team and I were ambushed in one of the most terrifying incidents I'd ever experienced. But as the bullets and grenades exploded into life around us, and in spite of our natural instinct to want to crawl up in the foot-wells of our vehicles, we realized that the only way we'd stand any chance of survival was to overcome the paralyzing fear and take the fight back to the enemy. I was convinced my team and I would probably all be killed, but when you're staring death in the face, it's amazing how natural the body's desire to survive really is. We took a deep breath, summoned up a deep, dark fury from the pits of our stomachs and violently fought fire with fire. Miraculously, we all managed to come out of it alive. But the next morning we had to go straight back out to deal with more bombs – and had to drive through the ambush site again. There wasn't time to get over the shock; it was truly unsettling. On reflection, not only did I realize that life is finite, I also realized the true importance of staying focused and keeping your sense of humor when things go pear-shaped."

How do you deal with stress?

"My stress levels were naturally at an all-time high when I was defusing bombs and IEDs. How did I learn to cope with it? In the surreal high-stakes, high-pressure world I was living in, where every decision could have been my last, I grew to learn that fear can be your friend. Confucius once said, 'Our greatest glory is not in never failing, but in rising each time we fail.' Instead of allowing fear to curtail success, you can use it to give you an edge. Visualizing a successful outcome and learning breathing techniques also helped!

During my career I pitted my wits against some of the world's most evil bombmakers. I personally began fighting against IRA bombmakers in 1999 – during my first EOD (Explosive Ordnance Disposal) tour in Northern Ireland. At the time they were considered to be the best in the world – but the level of technical sophistication they achieved in 30 years of fighting the British was superseded in just 12 months in Iraq and in 18 months in Afghanistan, and every time we went on the street, wherever we operated in the world, we were always being watched by the terrorists. They were constantly tracking our procedures. If they saw us walk straight up to a device – instead of clearing a safe route first, the next time they'd place a hidden secondary IED for sure. It was like a game of extreme chess, in which every move, every action was meticulously planned, and the consequences of those actions carefully weighed.

The 2005 London suicide bombings were a terrifying and traumatic situation. Managing to cope with the devastating scenes of carnage when I got there wasn't easy for anyone to face.

Lord Moran, who was Winston Churchill's physician, talked of soldiers having a stock of courage. Essentially, his theory was that people can be subjected to stress and trauma for a certain amount of time, but that each of us has a set 'level' of tolerance; and crucially, once that level runs down to a dangerous level, if we are withdrawn from the stressful environment immediately we can replenish it, but if we fail to do so in time, it reaches a critical level after which permanent damage sets in. During my career I witnessed countless traumatic incidents, and during my time as a young officer in Bosnia I reached that critical level. It's worth noting that more soldiers committed suicide after returning home from the Falklands than the 255 who were lost there in action. Twenty-four were killed in the first Gulf War – but seven times as many veterans have since taken their own lives. And there are more ex-military in prison, on parole, or serving community sentences than are currently deployed in Afghanistan. Post-traumatic stress disorder is a very real phenomenon.

But on the plus side we also become more resilient in time. The more we are exposed to stress and trauma, the more resilience we build up, and the higher our tolerance – or stock of courage – to it, becomes. That is what happened with me. I definitely witnessed far more traumatic experiences after Bosnia, in places such as Iraq, Afghanistan, and of course during 7/7. But by recognizing my critical levels of tolerance to stress, and by learning to rationalize what I witnessed and experienced, I have learnt to cope with virtually any traumatic experience that comes my way.

Another coping mechanism I've learnt is the ability to see the positives following a traumatic incident. I remember vividly on the evening of 7 July 2005, walking back along the Embankment, desperate to get home to my family, I thought of the images that flashed across the TV screens throughout the course of the day, and of those people who weren't going to make it home that night. I thought of the bravery, humility, and selflessness of all those passers-by who stopped to help and comfort the injured as they lay bleeding and dying, and I thought of the millions of calm, resigned Londoners who got on with their lives as four twisted fanatics tried to rob them of everything they cherished.

When I watch the news, return from a war-zone, or indeed speak with other friends who've recently returned from conflict, I realize that little changes. The world continues to be dangerous and unpredictable, and for the bomb disposal teams still operating, the switch continues to flick rapidly and repeatedly from full-off to full-on. But they love what they do. It's a vocation, a way of life. I've yet to meet a member of a bomb disposal team who isn't completely, intellectually, and spiritually absorbed by what he does. Operators desire only two things: to try to save the lives of the innocents, and to make it back home to their families. We're not men of the system. We're not even particularly interested in the cause. We're here to do a job.

That job was something I'd spent years training for. But being the victim of a violent ambush, and having to take the lives of others in the process, was an intense experience for me. It changes a man's life forever; how could it not? But I still believe it was all for the greater good. When I worked in intelligence, I had an American colleague who lived by a series of Christian principles. Fight what's wrong; believe what's true; do what's right. It's often a difficult path to follow, but one I still aspire to, and one that I continually advocate in my books and while giving motivational speeches.

The greatest, and certainly the most useful, lesson I learnt was the importance of being a good communicator, and having patience. Both were equally important in my role as an officer and bomb disposal operator. I also learnt a great deal of valuable lessons about leadership from the scores of amazing soldiers and officers that I worked with during my career.

The second is the importance of being relentless and not cutting corners. Unfortunately, as my team and I became more skilled at disabling terrorist bombs, the bombers became equally as skilled and determined – until the inevitable happened and I ended up with a price on my head. Although nothing focuses the mind quite like a death threat, I stayed alive ultimately because I didn't cut corners and I was relentless in seeing the task through to the end.

Finally, and in no particular order, I have learnt that embracing whatever challenges are thrown your way, and accepting rather than fearing change, goes a long way towards achieving success. So many people curtail their own success because they fear failure (and ridicule), but the fact is, most people are so absorbed in their own lives and dramas that they don't actually care what's going on in other people's lives. And besides, fear is healthy. It keeps you balanced and focused, but if you let it, it can also become an enemy to logic, which is why it's also important to rationalize the cause of your fears. Also, I always tell my audiences during my motivational talks to follow their gut instinct. I learnt the hard way to always listen to my gut instinct, and coupled with that have always held an intrinsic belief that I can and will succeed – given sufficient time and effort. If you believe you will succeed, listen to your gut instinct, and never lose sight of your aims, success will almost certainly follow.

I constantly learn from success and failure, but one of the greatest lessons I've learnt is to trust my intuition. Virtually every mistake in my life is as a result of failing to follow my intuition; conversely, every time I have ever followed it, the outcome has always been positive.

I have had numerous setbacks in my profession, far too many to list here, but one thing I learnt very early on is that wisdom and success are often gained through failure. Thomas Edison had 10,000 failures before successfully inventing the first working light bulb; and The Beatles were turned down by the Decca recording company who said they didn't like their sound and that guitar music was on its way out. On a personal level, when I've suffered my own setbacks and tried to look for a way out, I've always taken the time to make a plan, and crucially remembered the advice of an old Warrant Officer who mentored me as a young Russian linguist. He would always tell us: 'Don't look for the next opportunity … the one you have in hand is the opportunity.' People spend far too long waiting for something good to happen in their lives. I've never been a believer in the maxim 'All good things come to those who wait.' In my experience, all good things come to those who get off their arses and work hard trying to achieve their dreams.

I prioritize everything on a daily basis – whether it's time with my children, or work related. As far as I know we only get one life and prioritizing helps me get the most out of it. I've always believed that thorough planning will prevent the onset of most problems, but sometimes fate plays a part and there simply doesn't seem to be an obvious solution. When this happens, I embark on the start of the plan and wait for the variables to kick in so that I can adapt it accordingly – as events unfold. There's definitely a time for planning and a time for action, and people often fail because they fail to act at all.

Teamwork is the bedrock of success in the military. While we were on the assault course our color sergeant said to us: 'The only way you're going to get through this course, gentlemen, is through teamwork. No one can be a lone Jack here and succeed.' He was absolutely right. The assault course was the perfect place to identify people who were 'Jack.''At university, where most of the guys had spent the previous three years, many of them were encouraged to concentrate on their own academic development, but at Sandhurst it was a completely different dynamic. The focus was on the team and achieving the mission. Nothing else mattered.

The other thing I've learnt is always to attribute success to the team. It's amazing how much a team can accomplish when it doesn't matter who gets the credit! My work has always been more of a vocation than an occupation. I'm not sure people like me ever truly switch off from work. My career as a bomb disposal operator, and even now, as a counter-terrorism specialist, motivational speaker, and writer, often feels all-consuming. Perhaps the real question shouldn't be how we switch off from work when we're at home with our families, but rather how much of ourselves we leave behind.

Which situations on the battlefield caused me the most stress? Being ambushed and shot at was highly stressful, but every bomb I walked up to was stressful. As you take that long walk up to the IED, often carrying in excess of 150 lb of equipment, your pulse is racing and every sense is on full alert. You clear your mind of all the day-to-day nonsense like what you're going to have for dinner that night, what bills have to be paid, and how your team is doing in the league, and instead you focus solely on the bomb: where it is; how it might be constructed; and what the bombmaker who designed that attack is trying to achieve. Is he trying to kill innocent civilians; is he trying to kill the police or members of the security forces; or is he trying to kill me? The device might just be an obvious come-on that's been emplaced to lure me into the area so that I can be killed by something more sinister. In essence, you're playing a game of extreme chess with the bomber every time you take that long walk. But while you never think of death or failure – ever – in the back of your mind you have to maintain a healthy measure of paranoia … because at any moment you know that your time or luck could run out.

Then, when you reach the bomb, you can feel the drumbeat of your heart, rhythmically pounding away as you examine the bomb's circuitry, following the bird's nest loop of wires obsessively with your eyes until it makes sense. Only then can you cut into the deadly device and make it safe. Total failure, or complete success …

Shortly after we'd returned from a particularly harrowing tour of Bosnia during which 10,000 Muslims were massacred, I found myself suffering from post-traumatic stress disorder. I began to fall off the rails and was really starting to lose my way and question whether I was really making a difference and if I was worthy of leading soldiers at all. Brummie, my Troop Sergeant, gave me some amazing advice; he was a tough man who was no stranger to hardship. He'd spent time in a young offenders' institute and served with the elite French Foreign Legion, before joining the Pioneers, but despite his tough exterior, I soon realized that he was an extremely sensitive man who showed compassion and humility in abundance.

He sat and calmly listened to me as I struggled to articulate my anxieties, and then, having listened and taken in every word, he gave me some advice that has sustained me through every challenge I've ever faced since. He told me I'd never be able to solve all the world's problems in one go, but that it didn't mean I couldn't try to solve them one at a time. 'A lot of good men fail because they try too hard to be perfect', he said, 'And you know what? It's all right to be good. You can be a good enough husband, father, soldier, and still be a success.' I'll never forget those inspirational moments with him as he tried to shape me into a leader. Moreover, he taught all of us that worked with him that even in the macho culture of the Army, it's OK to be scared; through him we learnt the true meaning of courage: namely that courage isn't about never being scared; it's about having the ability to muster up the inner strength to overcome your fears when you are. He was a very wise man, and pretty soon I learnt – amongst other things – to rationalize the traumatic experiences I'd witnessed and in doing so, learnt to overcome fear and stress.

I always injected humor in a tense situation on the battlefield to relieve stress. During my time with the SAS, there were four over-arching tenets that formed the regimental ethos of that unit. They were: (1) The Unrelenting Pursuit of Excellence, (2) The Highest Standards of Self-Discipline, (3) A Classless Society, and (4) Humor and Humility. I've found all four to be indispensable in everyday life, but in particular the latter. Without frequent recourse to humor and humility, we stand the risk of taking ourselves far too seriously and of suffering from an unbecoming conceit and big-headedness, both of which are the antitheses of success.

My advice to people who find it difficult to cope with stress is to embrace whatever challenges are thrown your way and accept rather than fear change. This goes a long way towards alleviating stress. So many people curtail their own success because they fear failure and ridicule, but the fact is, most people are so absorbed in their own lives and dramas that they don't actually care. People shouldn't fear failure – challenges are exciting! They should listen to their gut instinct, believe they will succeed, never lose sight of their aims, and most importantly take time to rationalize whatever the cause of their stress and anxiety is. It's amazing how quickly and magically the stress disappears!

The most enjoyable aspect of my work as a bomb disposal expert was walking up to a terrorist bomb and neutralizing it. It is most definitely one of the most gratifying experiences imaginable. When you and your team witness the truly terrible effects of a terrorist bomb and the devastating effect it has on people's lives, it really is heartbreaking. But when one is found, and you are able to make it safe, and prevent that scene of carnage from re-occurring, there's no feeling like it. It's also one of the most exciting and adrenalin fuelled 'rushes' I've ever experienced, and those two aspects combined made it a potent and very addictive vocation."

ANALYSIS AND ADVICE

This interview provides a range of useful insights into stress management, and turning pressure into positive outcomes. First, the personal and professional experiences in life, particularly the more stressful and potentially psychologically disabling they are, the more you learn, whether it is the tragic loss of a family member, or seeing colleagues killed or damaged, or experiencing someone being badly treated by others. The "life lessons" are profound and can shape your ability to cope later in life.

Second, "overcoming paralyzing fearful events" can be a precursor to learning how to deal with less traumatic events because it enables you to contextualize the less severe forms of stress. By experiencing some of the worst pressures in life, you can look at the minor things that go wrong at work or in your family, and say to yourself "I need to put this into perspective. It is not like seeing a friend die in action or in a car crash, it is not life threatening, so calm down and look at the options to deal with it."

This leads to the third point: it might sound obvious, but people need to identify what underlies your "stress reaction" before being able to look at the options to deal with it. If you are feeling anxious or depressed, what is the source or cause of it at work, and what are the various options for dealing with it? This then involves exploring a cost–benefit analysis of each option, and ultimately selecting the one with the most benefits and least costs.

Fourth, it is better to take control of events rather than let them controlling you. Be patient, relentless in finding a solution and embracing the challenge to sort it out, rather than wallowing in the emotional mire.

chapter 4

Nikki King OBE – CEO, Isuzu Truck (UK) Ltd

Nikki King is a legend in the male-dominated motor industry, where she has been garlanded with numerous awards, including an OBE for services to the motor industry. She became Managing Director of Isuzu Truck (UK) Ltd in January 1996 when Isuzu Motors of Japan decided to enter the UK market and she has since grown it into a multi-million pound business.

She actively supports working mums, with over 50% of her senior management team being female. She is obsessive about her multi-award-winning customer care provision and this ethos runs throughout the entire company.

Nikki is also passionate about supporting and mentoring young people and is Chairman of the social enterprise charity Auto 22, an offshoot of Catch22 Social Enterprises. She was also instrumental in the creation of the Recovery Industry Support Charity.

In 2009 Nikki won a Lifetime Achievement Award at the First Women Awards in London. Her other achievements include an Honorary Doctorate from Staffordshire University and the Motor Transport Service to Industry Award for her outstanding contribution to the road transport industry.

She recently facilitated a complete buyout of Isuzu Truck UK by Isuzu Motors Japan, the third largest truck manufacturing company in the world.

The benefits to her staff are enormous and have provided them with a secure future with growth and opportunity for the company.

About Nikki

"I come from a long line of matriarchs. My grandmother ran six fish shops and trawlers in Grimsby from the late 1800s to her death in 1953. My mother was the driving force in our family restaurant/pub business and I had many aunts who over-achieved in a male dominated world. My life as a pub child gave me the 'never be rude to customers' ethos and the ability to talk to anyone about anything. I was an only child (my brother had been killed in a road accident ten years before I was born) with older parents who always treated me as an adult, which probably gave me an urge to achieve.

My father was from a privileged background and privately educated, and then joined the Indian Army as an officer. He gave me my sense of duty and responsibility for those who work for me and a great sense of morality. Mother was from a working class background – her father was a policeman and her mother a children's nanny. My father became a hopeless alcoholic and died aged 52, and mother took over the business reins.

As a child I was rebellious and did not focus on my academic career although I passed the 11+18 months early and went to grammar school at ten. This meant that intellectually I was able to achieve, but emotionally I was still two years younger than my peers. I loved languages and got A grades in English, French, and German. I failed miserably on everything else, then went to secretarial college and got a full B-Tech Business Studies Diploma, three A levels, and four O Levels in one year!

The 60s were a time of full employment so I walked straight into my first job as a bilingual secretary with no problem at all. My love of people and passion for customer service in a pub/restaurant definitely shaped my upbringing.

Before I was married I worked as a secretary. I went to work as PA to the Director of Joe Coral (Bookmakers) in Kent. I really loved the business and obtained the agreement from my boss that if I paid for my own training as a bookmaker (the company would not pay for a woman) they would reimburse me if I passed. Four years later I was managing their telephone account betting business and absolutely loved the job. I then left to get married.

I stopped work to bring up the children until finances made me take a part-time job. I ran Alan Knott's (England cricketer) benefit year and then took on a number of part-time secretarial roles.

I married a widower with two children (he was 23 years older than me) when I was 21. A year later our daughter was born and we were really hard up. When I was 40 and working as a part-time secretary, my husband left me for a family friend and left me penniless in an old, terraced house that was falling down around our ears. The divorce deal was that he took the money, paid no maintenance, and I got everything that ate – children (his and mine), dog, cats, and goldfish! It was actually very motivating.

When my marriage broke up I was forced to get a full-time job. I joined UDT (a finance company) as Office Manager. I have always said this was the most challenging management role of my career. I was headhunted a few years later by Ford Motor Credit and joined them as Assistant Branch Manager. I hated it and, after a year, was headhunted by an Iveco/Ford Dealer group in Kent to become their Fleet Administration Manager.

I fell in love with trucks at that point and began to help the salesmen when customers were in the dealership. Finally, I began to work as a Fleet Salesman and seven years later was Fleet Director and Managing Director of one of their locations.

This was during the recession of the 80s and I began to have doubts about whether the business would survive (it went down a year after I left). At that point, I was headhunted by the Lex Group to set up a multi-franchise 'one stop shop' fleet department for Lex Retail Group. Three years later, I was asked to set up Isuzu as a brand new business for Lex. After six years, as Lex was being sold off under the RAC banner, I led an MBO (management buyout) and we bought the business.

There were a number of challenges along the way. My first promotion to General Manager of the Fleet Department was marred when I was told I would have to have a male Sales Manager, as a woman was not capable of running a male sales team. Luckily, this man slipped a disc and was off work for three months, by which time I had proved he was not necessary and he was redeployed.

There were many times in my early career when suppliers ignored me as I was a 'mere woman', but I learnt to handle these situations and they became less and less of a problem.

There were also huge culture differences when I became MD of a Japanese company, and that is a book in itself! However, I freely admit I would not be where I am today without the support of a number of fantastic bosses and mentors.

It was a really tough call to bring in the first Japanese truck in the UK ever and the first new truck range for around 40 years. The UK truck market is very sophisticated and traditional so it was a very difficult market to break into.

The competition made a lot of hay around the fact I was a woman and said I would burn out in a year. However, I think it was completely to my advantage, as I am immediately recognizable in a room of 1200 men. Everyone knows me and I am often having conversations with men who think I know them and I have absolutely no idea who they are!

My Six Golden Rules for being successful in business are:

- Have a robust and tested vision and stick to it.
- Have enormous passion for your business and your vision.
- Be pragmatic and flexible.
- Always look at the future and constantly think of 'what ifs?'
- Surround yourself with people who are better than you and keep them motivated.
- Never forget who you are or get too big to be told of problems.

I have learnt from successes and failures and am still learning. The current recession has been a tremendous challenge to the business. The truck industry is the first into recession and the last out. Luckily, I saw this recession coming in 2007 and insisted that the Board prepared a doomsday scenario based on how we would prepare for recession, how we would know when it came, and what action we would take to combat the effects of the downturn. We shared this with our bankers at that stage and they thought we were mad. We immediately began to concentrate our sales and marketing on recession-proof business – food and drink, utilities, local authorities, rental, etc. – and took away our emphasis on construction, scaffolding, etc. This meant that when the recession came at the end of 2008, we were already much farther down the line than our competitors. We acted fast, cut costs in one hit, and survived. Also, our total commitment to customer service was a complete life saver at this time, as our customer retention remained constant.

When we began the business in 1996 with seven people, I promised them that if they worked hard they were guaranteed success. Then, out of loyalty and gratitude, they were promoted as the business grew, regardless of their attributes or capabilities. It took me ten years of pain to rectify this and was a big learning curve.

My best business investment was mortgaging everything to fund the MBO. At the time of the buyout, the Directors and General Managers (GMs) bought in, and all staff who worked for us at the time received share options. This was one of the best business decisions I ever made and really changed the culture of the company. I always said I was a corporate climber and not an entrepreneur, but maybe I was wrong and should have started many years earlier!

My people say that I am too quick to make decisions. They say I am right 80% of the time. Although not remotely spiritual or religious, I firmly believe in an inner voice. This voice told me when to buy the business and will probably tell me when to sell. I now surround myself with people who think hard and analyze everything and consult greatly before making a decision. I don't always listen to them but it is a great exercise.

My biggest success to date is that I'm still working for Isuzu! Since we began Isuzu there have been a number of newcomers who have all failed and retreated with bloody noses. We have won many international awards for Customer Service and our home developed CARE program is now being rolled out by Isuzu worldwide.

I am very careful not to overspend on fixed costs. We only employ additional people when the current staffing has been seriously overloaded for a significant period. Making family members redundant is a very painful experience for everyone, so I avoid it like the plague!

I like to practice what I preach and stay in Premier Inns when I am away on business – and my car is the cheapest on the fleet. I am a little more expansive on variable costs that can be switched off at a moment's notice.

I have a 'To Do' list that is with me 24/7. Every day I add to it and remove things I have achieved and prioritize and asterisk the task I must do. Every Friday, I work from home and concentrate on clearing as much of the list as I can.

We are always looking at ways to improve the service to our customers. Before any big initiative we hold a series of customer/dealer clinics to obtain positive feedback before we go to market. If we are considering a new role, we normally ask a Senior Manager to run with this until we are sure it has legs.

If I can't resolve a problem, I normally seek advice from my management team first. Then, I try to think of something I have experienced in my past that might help. I might call a mentor or friend who has relevant experience. I do a lot of my thinking in the car – I have a 60 mile journey to the office on the M25 so it gives me a great deal of thinking time! I also play computer games – for some reason this seems to help me concentrate.

We patent our ideas wherever possible. Our Customer Care Programme is our biggest USP. My people were horrified when I freely shared this with our competitors and helped one of them to copy it. I was convinced that while the process was easy, it is was really difficult to change the culture of a business to adapt to this obsession with customer service and I wanted to test the water – I am happy to say I was right and we now know this particular USP is impossible to copy.

I believe that good business partnerships are important. Everyone needs people who make up for their deficiencies, provide support, and share the passion and the vision.

Like all CEOs, I am always trying to achieve bigger targets; however, it's not an obsession. I firmly believe the dreaded phrase 'shareholder value' is totally responsible for the problems we currently face. Luckily, as a private company, we do not have that pressure. Our aim is to provide a great service to our customers and, by doing so, gradually increase our market share, but it is not the most important part of the business.

Timing is crucial in any business. Launching a new, bigger truck range in 2009 was terrible timing; however, Isuzu in Japan were the deciders of that so we had to run with it. Buying the business from Lex when they had taken the pain of losses in the startup years was great timing and I will always be grateful to them for the opportunity.

I keep an even work/life balance and I have always been able to switch off. It would have to be a really life-threatening problem for me to worry about it in my private time.

I never, ever look back. I try to learn from the experience and then I move on. I have never said 'I wish I had …' or 'I should have ….' This is just self-indulgent and pointless. I believe that the past is gone – the future is mine!

The business always comes first and I do not deserve friends. I never call them, I don't return calls, and I let them down at the last moment constantly! Fortunately, the friends I have are simply wonderful and put up with me. When I am out socially I never think about business or mention it. My daughter is a senior manager in the company and we have a firm rule that we never talk about business when we are at home.

I am now 65 so my opportunities for playing hard are minimal. The spirit is willing, but the flesh is now definitely weak! In my younger days I was a very hard player and I still believe that my people should 'work hard and play hard'. I never complain about expenses and truly believe some partying is vital for teamworking.

When it comes to coping with stress, I always use the 'What is the worst thing that can happen?' scenario. I think of the worst thing and how I would deal with it – then the next worse and so on. It always works as you realize the odds of a life-threatening outcome are very slim and you feel better when you have covered all eventualities.

I try to face difficult situations quickly and honestly. Much stress is self-inflicted because we will not fight dragons or deal with difficult situations. Because of my early life I know whatever happens I will survive and I always think of that if I am stressed out.

At the time of my divorce I began experiencing panic attacks when I was driving on the motorway. I simply couldn't overtake and be in the middle lane with cars either side of me. This got progressively worse until I couldn't drive at all. I had treatment from a great doctor and recovered, but am still prone to this when overtired or stressed. I have now developed a mantra that seems to help and keep the demons at bay. I am also terrified of flying, although I have to do this on numerous occasions – perhaps I am a control freak!!

The things that cause me the most stress:

• Cash flow issues during the recession.
• Disloyal members of staff.
• Letting my people down.

Qualities I look for in my employees:

– Expertise in their field.
– Passion for customer service.
– Loyalty.
– Rebelliousness.
– Thinking outside the box.
– Ability to go the extra mile.
– Sense of fun and humor.
– Good interpersonal skills (except IT and Finance – not always easy to find!).

If they don't meet their targets, I look carefully to see if the target is unreasonable. Then I look to see if mentoring or training is needed. I give as much help as possible. However, if the person is incompetent I look to see if another role is more suitable. If not, I begin the process of replacing them.

I am very heavily involved in recruitment. My managers choose someone on their ability to do the job, but either myself or another Director conducts a final interview to see if they fit culturally.

My advice to budding business entrepreneurs is to form a robust vision you are passionate about. Never deviate from the vision or lose the passion, and network, network, network!!!

Probably the one thing I would change if I had to do it all again is to think about an exit route much earlier. Now I am 65 I realize there is a great deal to do before I can exit this business with enough money to retire or do something else and protect the business and my team going forward. Exiting well and effectively is the final piece in the jigsaw and most people ignore it until it is too late."

ANALYSIS AND ADVICE

Once again we can see how early childhood experiences can create a resilient personality, and how events along the life cycle can create an individual's coping strategies. In terms of the latter, we are seeing more and more women entrepreneurs and senior managers talk about being "a woman in a man's world" and how that has affected them in dealing with the inevitable obstacles.

There are a range of generic points that one can raise here about dealing with workplace and other issues. First, have a sense of purpose, a vision, and passion and not divert from it. Second, which we have heard elsewhere, be pragmatic and flexible in the wake of constant workplace and social change.

Third, and something that a number of successful people have suggested, "stay rooted," don't believe your own press, and never get too big to be told problems at work or to be open to other people's constructive criticisms. This is easily done as a person moves up the success hierarchy.

Fourth, be in tune with your "inner voice," be aware of your weakness and respond from who you are, not your role.

Fifth, and probably from an effective stress coping perspective, never look back and say "I wish I had ..." or "I should have ..."; learn from your mistakes but don't dwell on them.

The people who get ahead in life are those that have a "bounce-back" mentality—their self-talk would be something like 'I have failed, I will learn from this and then get on with the next venture without wallowing in the failure'. As Woody Allen once humorously wrote about taking 'work' too seriously: "I don't want to achieve immortality through my work, I want to achieve it by not dying."

And finally, always ask yourself the following question after any setback at work or in life, "What is the worst thing that can happen?" – most problems and stresses are not life-threatening.

chapter 5

Frederick Forsyth CBE – International Bestselling Author, Journalist, and Political Commentator

Frederick Forsyth is an English author, journalist, and occasional political commentator. He is best known for thrillers such as The Day of the Jackal, The Odessa File, The Fourth Protocol, The Dogs of War, The Devil's Alternative, The Fist of God, Icon, The Veteran, Avenger, The Afghan, The Cobra *and* The Kill List, *to name but a few.*

The son of a furrier, Frederick was born in Ashford, Kent. He was educated at Tonbridge School and later attended the University of Granada in Spain. Before becoming a journalist, he joined the RAF and was a jet fighter pilot. He joined Reuters in 1961 and later the BBC in 1965, where he served as assistant diplomatic correspondent.

Frederick's early career was spent covering French affairs and the attempted assassination of Charles de Gaulle. As a BBC correspondent, he was assigned to report on the Nigerian Civil War between Biafra and Nigeria, and he was there from the beginning in July 1967. Few expected the war to last very long considering the poor weaponry and preparation of the Biafrans when compared to the British-armed Nigerians. After three months, Frederick was recalled to London. In February 1968, eager to see what had happened, he asked the BBC to let him go back with a group from the British media. The mission was refused. He took leave and went privately to discover everything he said would happen was happening.

Frederick returned to Biafra as a freelance reporter, writing his first book,
The Biafra Story, in 1969. After his return, from 1970 onward, he became a
full-time novelist and on 16 February 2012, the Crime Writers' Association
announced that he had won its Cartier Diamond Dagger award in
recognition of his body of work.

About Frederick

"I was born in August 1938 in Ashford, Kent, which back then was a small
market town. My parents were both shopkeepers and jointly ran a shop.
On the ground floor there was a woman's dress shop, which my mother
ran, and upstairs there was a fur salon, which my father was in charge of.
They did this until they retired in the mid-60s. They were not wealthy but
comfortable – and I would say middle of middle class – and I would class
them as entrepreneurial to have been running shops in those days.

I grew up in a very loving family and was sent to a boarding prep school
at the age of nine. When I was about 12, they said they couldn't afford to
send me there unless I got a scholarship, so I worked extremely hard and
eventually got my scholarship to Tonbridge School. Whilst I was there,
I got intensively bullied because I was regarded as a swot as I was a scholarship boy. I was in a sports-crazy house and a swot was something you
kicked. This made me withdraw into myself and I have been reasonably
solitary ever since.

I wasn't very academic, but my parents were keen that I learnt about
Europe. My father had been through the war, ending as a Major, and he
was keen that his only son should know something about Europe. He was
a member of the Rotary Club and they had a twinning with a town in
France. My parents sent me there on an exchange for eight weeks during the summer months every year from the age of nine. By the time
I was 13, I was bilingual in French, then did the same in Germany for
three consecutive years. I got into Tonbridge School by getting a Modern
Language scholarship.

I came out of school with only one ambition and that was to fly. From a young boy I had always been mad on planes and my bedroom was surrounded by everything to do with planes. I decided I wanted to join the Air Force, but I was too young so I went to Spain and became quadrilingual in Spanish, then came back and wangled my way into the Air Force. I did my two years' service and got my wings flying jets. I was asked to stay on, but as they couldn't guarantee to assign me to Hunter squadron I decided to leave and indulge in my second ambition, which was to travel. My Dad gave me every encouragement to travel, even though his contemporaries were getting their sons to help in their businesses. I wondered how I could afford to travel around the world and thought I would become a Foreign Correspondent. I went straight from the Air Force into journalism and became a cub reporter for a newspaper in Norfolk. After three years, I joined Reuters in Fleet Street and had a series of lucky breaks. The first was getting sent to their Paris office to cover the various attempts by the Extreme Right OAS to assassinate Charles de Gaulle. I was then posted to East Berlin at the age of 25 at the height of the Cold War. This was extremely challenging and very interesting. I had a privileged career with Reuters, then joined the BBC.

The media have never paid reporters much money. I had a one-room bedsitter with a single gas ring in Kings Lynn, Norfolk, and shared a bathroom. I was never poor, but at the same time I was never wealthy. You don't make any money in journalism, but I managed to get by.

I never envisaged being a professional writer. I went out to cover the Nigerian Biafra war on the basis of a flat assurance that it would be over in a month. In fact it went on for several years and tragically cost the lives of about a million children. When I came back I had no job and no prospects of getting one. I had to think what I was going to do next. I thought that if I wrote a novel, it would be a quick way to earn some money. My friends disagreed, saying it was no way to make money, as the chances of getting it published were remote. Being stubborn, I went ahead and my first thought was to write a book about Paris and a contract killer. In those days, contract killers were unheard of. For that reason, I didn't think my book, *The Day of the Jackal*, would take off; nor did the publishers. Fortunately, it sold well and the publishers wanted me to write another one. For my next novel, I thought back to my days in Germany and then wrote *The Odessa File* about a shady organization that looked after ex-Nazis called ODESSA in Germany. My third novel, set back in Africa, was called *The Dogs of War*. After that book, I effectively ceased being a Foreign Correspondent and became a novelist, which is what I have been for the last 40 years.

After the first three books, I got tagged with the reputation for intensive research into the darker areas of what the establishment was up to when the lights went out. The hardest novel to write was *The Fist of God*, as I wasn't able to go out to Iraq. I had a man out there who gave me all the inside knowledge and I had to rely on interviewing people who had been in Iraq. It was a very complicated, multi-layered book with five different plots going on.

I rarely get stressed, as I have an optimistic attitude to life. What's the point of worrying about things that can't be changed, especially if they are way beyond my power to change? If things go wrong, I shrug them off and either junk the idea or try to solve the problem by doing it a different way. My advice to people suffering with stress is to avoid taking pills, unless you have to for medical reasons. Far too many people rely on them. I used to smoke, which had a calming effect, and I was a bit tetchy for a year after I stopped 12 years ago. I am pretty easy-going, which helps me to avoid stress.

I write a book about every three years, but not because I work on them for three years. I start off with the idea then mull over it and do some basic research to see if it's feasible, then if it is I will do it. I initially devise the story, then, during seven to eight months of intense research, travel to places that are going to be in the book, followed by 48 days of writing, which all takes about a year.

I would say the key point in being successful as an author is that whatever you write has to be of interest. My writing mainly appeals to men, the majority being middle aged, who think they have boring jobs. I am basically saying to them that they can come with me backstage where I will show them politicians without their make-up, how the special effects are accomplished, and what the sets look like. This behind-the-scenes style of writing seems to be of interest, especially to the people who don't have that kind of life. I do a lot of research in order to get it right. I think a book should be readable, interesting and well-researched, and set out in layman's language.

Although all my books have sold well, I did write a book once that wasn't as successful. It was when Andrew Lloyd Webber asked me to write a sequel to *Phantom of the Opera*. I mulled it over, as it was a challenge as I don't do romance or love stories. I decided to write it and unfortunately it didn't sell. Some felt it was too short and others bought the book having noticed my name on the cover. When they discovered it wasn't another spy story, they were naturally disappointed. To make matters worse, when the musical *Love never Dies* came out, Lloyd Webber changed the plot completely, so I couldn't even sell the book on the back of the play.

I tend to research so meticulously that when I sit down to write it's already finished and in my head; then all I have to do is put the words on paper. I have all the research in piles in a horseshoe shape around me. For example, if I had to write a scene involving the flight deck of a Jumbo 747, I would have talked at some length to the Captain of a Jumbo 747 and made a huge amount of notes about it, which I could then use when I needed to write about that subject.

I find it hard to switch off when I'm writing a book. I tend to write from about 7:00 a.m. to midday, then have lunch. I then go back to work until early evening and then switch off before going to bed. I go back to writing the next morning so my thoughts are hardly broken. As a journalist, you get used to writing to a deadline and I actually write better with a bit of pressure. My wife, Sandy, will not converse with me when I'm writing a book, as she knows that my mind will be elsewhere. When the book is written, I become a normal human being again. I do all my work by typewriter and don't have a computer.

During the writing year, I rarely socialize and seldom go out unless I am pushed to go out for an evening. I tend to write six days a week and allow myself one day off, so if I do go out, it will be on the night before my day off.

I have never written books with other authors as I prefer to work on my own. On a couple of occasions I have spent days with someone who has a great knowledge of something I need to describe in the book; however, I would not call them paid researchers.

A lot of youngsters write to me about becoming authors. I advise them not to expect to write a bestseller at the age of 18 as you need to know a bit about life and learn something about the world around you. I prefer to write about what I know: that's why I don't write romance, fantasy, or science fiction, as I couldn't begin to know how to write about a schoolboy with specs who is also a sorcerer.

If I started all over again, I would certainly join one of the armed forces. I would most probably still want to be a journalist as I enjoy travelling, and possibly emigrate to Australia, with its enviable beaches and all-year sunshine. I think you have to give everything in life your best shot. If it works you're lucky and if it doesn't, don't let it destroy you."

ANALYSIS AND ADVICE

You can see how the early and later life experiences can influence one's personality and coping strategies later in life. When one experiences problems at school or is confronted by stressful/traumatic events in your early career, they can have a profound effect on you and how you approach potentially stressful events later in life. These early life events can make you put the other more mundane, everyday pressures into context. We see this referred to time and time again in our interviews: that early or traumatic experiences can make current minor pressures less stressful and more easily dealt with.

Several generic points come out of this for us. First, there is the point about contextualizing all your worries and asking yourself the question "Is this life-threatening?," and if not, try to find a solution to it in as rational and analytical way as possible.

Second, if it is a problem you can't possibly deal with on your own (e.g. the downward spiral of the economy, or the war in Afghanistan), then forget about it and "concentrate on the things you can change." There is much you can change in the workplace (for example, how hard or long you work, career planning, team building with colleagues), but worrying about whether your organization will go bust in a recession is outside your control. On the other hand, if your organization is in financial difficulties, and you rationally think it could go under, then you should begin to think through your options for the future.

Trying to change something in your workplace or in society is extremely difficult, so concentrate on those things you can change. As Machiavelli wrote in *The Prince*:

> It should be borne in mind that there is nothing more difficult to arrange, more doubtful of success and more dangerous to carry through than initiating change. The innovator makes enemies of all those who prospered under the old order, and only lukewarm support is forthcoming from those who would prosper under the new

And finally, given life is a one-act play, give it, as Forsyth suggests, "your best shot, if it works you're lucky and if it doesn't don't let it destroy you." Again we need to learn from failure but not embrace it!

Dr. David Dunaway – Surgeon, Great Ormond Street Children's Hospital, London

David Dunaway graduated from the University of Manchester in 1989 and became a Fellow of the Royal College of Surgeons in 1992. He undertook his higher surgical training in plastic surgery in Leeds, Newcastle, London and at the Australian Craniofacial unit in Adelaide. He is also qualified as a dentist and is a Fellow Dental Surgeon of the Royal College of Surgeons.

In 1996 he became a consultant Plastic Surgeon at Canniesburn Hospital in Scotland, where his specialist interests were in facial deformity and head and neck surgery.

In July 2000, David was invited to join the Plastic Surgery and Craniofacial Unit at Great Ormond Street Hospital for Children. He now leads the craniofacial service. He is also a member of the adult craniofacial service based at University College London Hospital and the Eastman Dental Hospital.

His principal academic interests are in the study of the functional aspects of syndromic craniosynostosis and the correction of congenital facial deformity. He has published widely on frontofacial distraction osteogenesis.

In his private practice, David undertakes most aspects of cosmetic and reconstructive facial surgery and he has a special interest in facial rejuvenation and rhinoplasty. David takes an active role in training young plastic surgeons in cosmetic and reconstructive surgery. He lectures regularly, and participates in training organized through the Royal College of Surgeons, BAPRAS and the Royal Society of Medicine. He has an international practice in the treatment of craniofacial. Other interests include the management of vascular malformations and skin lesions.

David is a past president of the plastic surgery section of the Royal Society of Medicine and is secretary general of the European Society of Craniofacial Surgeons. He is actively involved in teaching surgeons in Africa and is a trustee of Facing Africa, a British charity treating children from Third World countries with craniofacial deformity.

About David

"I was born in Hampstead and my parents were comfortable middle class, but not wealthy. My mother didn't work and my father was an architect.

I have two younger sisters and my memories of childhood are of a loving, cohesive supportive family. I was never aware of any childhood events that may have affected me.

Having said that, I think I was an easy-going child and content with my lot. I wasn't particularly academic.

I went to a secondary modern school in Southgate, London, due to my lack of academic enthusiasm at primary school. My parents were not in a position to privately educate me; however, my mother constantly encouraged me to do the best I could and encouraged my growing interest in science which I excelled at school.

In my third year of secondary school, I was transferred to our local Grammar School.

Throughout secondary school, my interest in study and the world increased. My father was a great sounding board, although we disagreed about politics, religion, and life in general. In my later teenage years, our relationship became strained and took about 20 years to fully mend our relationship. My mother has remained a major support and to this day offers forthright views on how best to approach life.

I was hard up when I was a medical student and started a family. My wife Sue is a nurse and worked as a theatre sister to support us. Having previously qualified as a dentist, I was able to do some part-time work in dental practice, but money was very tight. Our lives were very busy and my study and work left very little family time. Once I had qualified as a doctor our lives were very much driven by my ambition to succeed, which meant that we moved a great deal so that I could obtain the best possible training.

I can remember times when we were very broke and even affording the weekly food bill was difficult. I don't think money has ever been a motivation for success. Now that we are financially comfortable, I enjoy the feeling of security this brings, but neither Sue nor I are particularly extravagant in our tastes (except for the money we spend on travel).

My motivation to succeed is I think to do as well as I can at my job. I really enjoy being an innovator and leading a good team.

I decided I wanted to do medicine in the fifth year of secondary school and worked hard for my exams. I went to UCH London in 1974 to study medicine, but failed the first year exams and was thrown out. I don't think I had really worked what I wanted to do and I think I was too immature to study independently at university. This failure was a real shock to me and it was at this time that I realized that, to achieve anything useful, I was going to have to apply myself and work hard.

I went to work as a lab technician for Ever Ready batteries in their analytical lab. At the time they were trying to work out how to make effective NiCd rechargeable batteries. Although the work I was doing was quite menial, I really enjoyed being involved with a team trying work out the science behind these batteries. I thought about applying to study chemistry, but in the end applied to study dentistry.

The dental school at UCH agreed to take me despite my dismal attempts at the first year in medicine. I think I was quite a good dental student and

I certainly enjoyed dentistry. This may be just my perception though. At our 25-year dental school reunion, I met with many people I hadn't seen for some time. Most of them seem quite surprised that I had gone on to develop a new career requiring so much work and application.

After qualifying in dentistry, I worked in hospital jobs and particularly enjoyed oral surgery. I met my wife-to-be whilst working at the North Staffs Royal Infirmary. By then, it had become clear that I really wanted a job in surgery and that the only way forward would be to study medicine. I was well supported by the hospital consultants I worked for and so I applied to study medicine again. Perhaps more surprising was support from Sue my then wife.

I studied medicine in Manchester. This time round I applied myself whole-heartedly to the task of studying. At the end of the first year, I won a scholarship, which paid my fees for my medical training. Studying, earning a living and making a pitifully small amount of time available to help bring up our family took up all of the hours in every day.

I qualified in 1989 and went on to do some very busy junior doctor's jobs. These were the days before the European working time directive and it wasn't uncommon to work 100 hours a week. I can remember working for a professional surgical firm in South Manchester and twice a month I would be on call, working from Thursday morning until the following Tuesday morning. I think this pressure of work was very harmful to personal and family life and I am lucky that we survived it as a cohesive family. Having said that, the experience left me a changed person: far more determined and conscientious, better equipped to work as hard as is needed to get a job done, and well equipped to deal with large amounts of stress.

My training in plastic surgery involved a lot of travelling and even more hard work. I trained under some great mentors in Leeds, Bradford, Newcastle, Great Ormond Street and the Australian craniofacial unit in Adelaide. The most informative time was undoubtedly my fellowship in Adelaide. David David, who headed the unit, is a giant of craniofacial surgery. I hope he won't mind me referring to him as a despotic leader. He was a very clear thinker and a great teacher. I think he may have recognized some potential in me and he spent a considerable amount of time explaining and discussing his thoughts. At the end of the year, I had a very clear view of his surgical philosophy, which still underpins my views today. He also insisted that I was on call for the craniofacial unit every day and night, so along with clear thinking, I gained an enormous amount of surgical experience.

After completing my training, I took up a consultant job in plastic surgery at Canniesburn Hospital in Glasgow, where our family home remains to this day. David Soutar was the senior head and neck plastic surgery consultant. His surgical wisdom was another great influence in developing my own skills.

In 2000, I moved to the Craniofacial Unit in Great Ormond Street, which is my dream job. The team at Great Ormond Street and I made headline news all round the world in August 2011 when we successfully separated conjoined twins Rital and Ritag Gaboura. People ask how I coped with the pressure of this difficult operation. It was all down to a matter of careful research and planning, as well as seeking the opinions of trusted and respected colleagues, which helped reduce the stress.

By the end of the planning stage, we had a very good idea about the problems we would face and had worked out a strategy of relatively simple steps. By staging the operation, the procedure was simplified and the risk reduced. As far as possible we had also planned 'defensive manoeuvres' for each major stage which would protect the twins from serious harm if we ran into unexpected problems.

There was no media coverage until the twins were separated, so there were no media distractions around the surgery. I expected to find the media attention stressful, but it wasn't.

My six key points in being successful in whatever field you work are:

1. Practice. Work hard and get lots of experience
2. Knowledge. Read about your subject
3. Work well with other people and treat them fairly

4. Luck
5. Reflection. Know your strengths and weaknesses
6. Aptitude for what you are doing. You don't have to be the best at all aspects of your job, but some natural skill is necessary.

I have learnt from successes and failures. Successes should be built upon. Failures should be regarded as your own fault. Never blame bad luck and always reflect on what you could have done to achieve a better outcome or avoid failure.

My main setbacks were getting through examinations, which I kept taking until I passed. My higher surgical training was rapid, with well-respected trainers, and my consultant career has been in excellent, well-resourced units.

Apart from separating the conjoined twins, my team and I introduced frontofacial distraction osteogenesis to treat children with craniosynostosis. This is what I am best known for in craniofacial surgery.

I also lead a surgical team on a visit to Ethiopia each year, where we undertake complex facial reconstructions on children affected by noma.

I try to prioritize on a daily basis and work through the most important tasks. I am usually too busy to complete everything, so some tasks get delayed. However, they get completed as soon as I have time. Unexpected tasks or problems do not unduly worry me.

I enjoy taking on new challenges and like to fit them into a reasonably defined working week timetable. If I get stuck in a rut and can't resolve a problem, I take a run. I find it's an excellent time to think and hopefully resolve any problems or issues. Most apparently insolvable problems can, with some thought, be broken down into a series of solvable problems.

Brainstorming sessions with large numbers of people do not suit me. I find a much better strategy is to sit and quietly talk through various aspects of a problem with small numbers of people. I find large meetings useful when a consensus is required.

Teamwork is extremely important in my work. Well-functioning teams generally solve problems more effectively than individuals, and it is good to have a balanced skill mix. Good teams are also able to be effectively self-critical and having many people involved helps prevent mistakes.

I never completely switch off from work, although I am getting better at 'switching off' as I get older. I work five or six days a week and between 50 and 70 hours in a normal week.

My work rarely affects my sleep. I occasionally lose sleep over bad days, but the everyday ups and downs of work don't affect my mood very much.

I don't have an even work/life balance. My wife and family have learnt to accept this and we have introduced some work-free times during the week to try to address the intrusion of work into the home. Holidays away from work influences are an important part of our year.

The things I find most stressful are not having the ability to act on a problem, either through a lack of understanding of the issues, or not having the authority, tools, or knowledge to deal with the problem. My strategy, if I have one, is to be forewarned, have a plan, avoid stressful problem overload, obtain the necessary skills and knowledge, and perhaps most importantly, engage the help and support of others.

The situations that cause me the most stress at work include not having enough time to deal with a problem satisfactorily, or having to rely on other people who I feel are incompetent especially in urgent situations. I find being able to do something toward solving the problem in a stressful situation helps enormously.

What do I look for in people who work with me? I look for diligent, hard-working, knowledgeable people with good clinical acumen and a good understanding of their limitations. Team players are an advantage, but not all members of a team need to be good collaborators.

If people fail to reach targets, it is good to understand why. They may have been asked to do an impossible job, or there may be external circumstances preventing them from achieving. A good team leader will help to address these issues. In my experience, most people want to perform well at work. Lazy, unenthusiastic people should, if possible, be bypassed and encouraged to find jobs that suit their skills. I am easily accessible to staff who work at the hospital, which puts everyone at ease. I think humour is a good way of defusing tense situations and an effective tool for communicating your point of view.

The enjoyment of my work is treating and helping patients, especially children, who make the best patients. I also like the challenge of solving complex surgical problems and clinical research, particularly my work on frontofacial advancement, which has made a significant contribution to craniofacial surgery, including my work on the analysis of 3D facial images."

ANALYSIS AND ADVICE

Again we see that some setbacks in life can be a great motivator, but there are plenty of lessons to learn from the pressures of a surgeon. First, it is vital to have a good working relationship with your colleagues, and to treat them fairly because, down the line, they can be your social support system when you need support either at work or personally. Second, it is important to be able to prioritize your work and other aspects of your life. Stress occurs frequently when people fail to deal with the important things in their lives or work, and let the less pressing or "easy to do" stuff to take priority – usually because these are less complex or involve less emotionality or are less painful to do.

Third, in dealing with what appears to be insolvable problems, it is best to break them down into smaller solvable parts, which provides you with the self-confidence to deal with the bigger picture down the line.

Fourth – a theme we have heard about from others in this book – learn from your failures, or as Confucius wrote "our greatest honour is not in never failing, but in rising every time we fall." And then make sure you are in a job you love that provides you with purpose, or again, as Confucius reflected, "choose a job that you like and you will not have to work a day in your life."

And finally, stay away from "glass half empty" people. They are a drain on your emotional resources and at work are a major source of stress. The best advice we have come across here is from Mark Twain, who once wrote "Keep away from people who try to belittle your ambitions. Small people always do that, but the really great make you feel that you, too, can somehow become great."

chapter 7

Gian Fulgoni – Co-Founder and Executive Chairman, comScore, Inc.

Gian M. Fulgoni has been the Chief Executive Officer of Lancaster Enterprises LLC since November 1998. He is Co-Founder of comScore, Inc. (aka Comscore Networks Inc.) and has been its Executive Chairman since September 1999. Gian has more than 30 years of leadership experience and is the recipient of numerous industry awards, including Illinois Entrepreneur of the Year and the Wall Street Transcript Award for outstanding contributions as Chief Executive Officer of Information Resources, Inc. In 2008, Gian was inducted into the Chicago Entrepreneur Hall of Fame. He was educated in the UK, and holds an MA in Marketing from the University of Lancaster and a BSc in Physics from the University of Manchester.

About Gian

"I was born in South Wales in 1948 to Italian parents who had immigrated to the UK shortly before World War II. My father owned and operated a small café/restaurant in Pontypool that he had started in partnership with his brother. My parents were adamant that I (and my siblings) not follow them into the restaurant business, but rather get a good education and be able to 'make something of ourselves'. I was raised with a lot of discipline (that was difficult to accept at times, but

I now see the value of it) and taught that hard work and a good education are necessary to be successful in life.

My parents were entrepreneurial and very hard working. I don't think I was ever hard up, but certainly, when I was a student and later when I first started working, my financial resources were limited. I was raised with a burning desire to be successful in my chosen career and to build wealth. My parents taught me that with an education and hard work anything was possible.

I studied hard and have a high IQ with strong quantitative and qualitative skills so I was able to attend a top-notch high school and from there to be admitted to the University of Manchester, where I graduated with a BSc Hons degree in Physics in 1969, and later Lancaster University, where I obtained an MA in Marketing in 1970. While studying at Manchester I had realized that I did not have any 'competitive advantages' in physics and that, in fact, I did not desire a career in the field. I concluded that a combination of my quantitative skills coupled with a marketing degree would open new and exciting career opportunities for me in the business world. Things worked out as I had hoped.

In 1970, the field of marketing was new and my marketing degree was viewed as unique. In conjunction with my strong quantitative abilities (as evidenced by my physics degree) my MA in Marketing was directly responsible for my being offered an entry-level position with Management Science Associates, Inc. (MSA), a young market research company in Pittsburgh, PA. As a result, I moved to the US from the UK in 1970 and my career has been built in the US since then.

In some ways, being raised in the 1950s and 60s in a small Welsh town by Italian parents who wanted me to retain their Italian culture was not easy. Being seen to be different is a challenge, particularly in high school. I worked hard at being accepted socially and academically while studying very hard in an effort to rank at the top of my class. I learnt the importance of humor in being accepted in social situations, to never give up and that, with hard work, anything is possible. I believe this helped give me the discipline and skills I have leveraged throughout my business career.

I have typically worked in, or founded, start-up market research companies, focused on building new measurement services that are enabled by technological breakthroughs. I take great pride in building market measurement capabilities that never previously existed or that some had even said would not be possible.

I did not work in a variety of jobs at the start of my career. In fact, I remained with MSA (my first employer) for a decade, learning the ins and outs of market research. This encompassed the collection, computer processing and analysis of data, and how to manage client projects. I also honed my sales and presentation skills. I worked my way up the corporate ladder and was at the EVP level when I left in 1980 to join Information Resources, Inc. (IRI), an exciting start-up company that had harnessed the power of point-of-sale scanner data to measure consumer buying behavior with an accuracy and timeliness never before possible.

When I obtained my Masters in marketing, it was clear to me that I was going to pursue a career in either brand marketing or market research. I finished second in my MA class and with my strong quantitative/analytical skills, I was recommended by the head of the Lancaster MA program for an entry-level position with MSA in Pittsburgh. When the opportunity came along to work in the US in market research, I jumped at it, since the US was home to the best in marketing. Market research has been my chosen field ever since.

Today, I am the Executive Chairman of comScore, Inc., a position I have held since co-founding the company in September 1999.

There is always stress when one is working for a fast-growing, ambitious, public company such as comScore. The stress comes from:

- Having to meet quarterly revenue and profit targets.
- Having to continuously develop new products and services in a dynamic, fast-changing industry.
- Having to satisfy demanding clients.
- Having to find, hire, and retain top-notch people in a very competitive industry.

– Having to travel extensively on a global basis to meet with key clients and to speak at numerous high-visibility conferences."

How do you cope with stress?

"Having experienced such challenges previously at another public company (IRI) helps me understand the challenges at comScore and gives me confidence that I can deal with them. This reduces stress. Having an experienced senior management team that willingly meets its challenges is also critically important. I find that regular exercise at the beginning of the day is a vital benefit. I try to run three to five miles first thing every day and I find that this relaxes me mentally and physically for the day's challenges. Finally, I've found that a good night's sleep of seven to eight hours is a great stress reducer.

I have more than 40 years of leadership experience and have held either the President, CEO or Chairman position at two public companies. I put my success down to:

– Leveraging changes in technology that create opportunities to introduce radically new services.
– Having strong analytical skills.
– Being able to persuasively 'sell' my ideas.
– Surrounding myself with top-notch people who are at least as smart as I am and hopefully smarter.
– Working hard and relentlessly.
– Being a good communicator – internally and externally – and being able to energize and motivate a team to accomplish extraordinary things.
– Being flexible in strategic direction.

I take my work problems home with me and find it difficult not to do so. Being able to reflect on a problem at my leisure often helps me come up with a solution.

I am the proud recipient of a number of notable industry awards, including being named an Ernst & Young Entrepreneur of the Year, twice being named Illinois Entrepreneur of the Year – the only person to have twice received that honor – and receiving the Wall Street Transcript Award for outstanding contributions as Chief Executive Officer of IRI. I am proud of all my achievements, especially in 2008 when I was inducted into the Chicago Entrepreneurship Hall of Fame, and in 2012 when I received an Honorary Fellowship from the University of Glamorgan in Wales.

My career has been spent growing start-up companies that leveraged technological dislocations, so my biggest challenges tend to have a common characteristic – how to persuade clients that my company's new solutions are needed and/or are superior to those of their incumbent suppliers. This, of course, entails building the actual solutions, and then persuasively communicating to prospective clients the manner in which technology is likely to change the way that business is done – and why my company's new solutions are needed if a client is to remain competitive or to gain a competitive advantage.

Because I'm ambitious and see many opportunities, it's easy for me to get overloaded. I could be a better scheduler/manager of my personal time, but I willingly devote as much time as is needed by the task at hand to meet deadlines. As a result, I get tasks accomplished on time, but probably with more stress than if I was able to plan my personal time better.

I am Executive Chairman of comScore and fortunate to work with a top-notch CEO (and my co-founder) who handles most of the company's day-to-day issues and who is also a brilliant product innovator, allowing me to focus my time on the development of various product lines, client development, and building/promoting the comScore brand. That's not to say that I don't get stressed. I do, but I accept it as a fact of life and I've developed ways with which to deal with it.

The 'great recession' of 2009 had a negative effect on comScore's profits, as it did for most companies. Thankfully we have recovered and we are once again growing strongly.

I would say the six key points to being successful in business are:

1. Understanding and leveraging one's true competitive advantages.
2. Being relentlessly competitive and hard working.

3. Having excellent persuasive communication skills.
4. Being flexible.
5. Being able to make fast decisions.
6. Having technical knowledge/familiarity and strong analytical skills.

I have learnt from successes and failures, but I've found that most people tend to learn more from failures than successes. Failures make you carefully examine what went wrong and you learn from it. Successes are often easy to take for granted.

My biggest business setback was having the US Justice Dept block the acquisition of IRI by Dunn & Bradstreet in 1987 on anti-competitive grounds (D&B owned the AC Nielsen company – IRI's #1 competitor). It left IRI in a vulnerable financial position with revenue growth stalled and negative cash flow. My challenge was re-energizing the business as a standalone company and making sure that employees were focused and motivated, and that they believed IRI would recover and succeed. Leadership, persuasive/motivating communication and hard work were the keys.

I take risks in business and sometimes base my decisions on gut instinct. I think taking risks and making gut feel decisions are natural parts of building a business from scratch."

What makes for business success?

"My biggest business successes to date have been building IRI and comScore from start-ups into large, successful, public companies. In the case of IRI, I led it to become the largest US market research company, with revenues in excess of $500 million per year and a market cap at its peak of $1.5 billion. All this was whilst successfully competing against the AC Nielsen company, a much larger, established competitor with deep pockets.

Careful budgeting of revenue and costs is a vital fact of life for any company. Like many, I find that it's a lot easier to predict costs than to forecast sales. I do believe that it's important not to have all of one's eggs in one product basket or one strategy. Even the best strategic planner cannot predict all of the unexpected changes in their surrounding market that might occur and which could eliminate the potential success of a single product or strategy.

It's easy for me to try to do too much, but I *never* miss deadlines. This does, however, increase my stress level more than it might need to be. However, I will gladly spend as much time as is required to address something unexpected that comes along if it's relevant to the success of the business.

I only implement work changes if the new process can reduce costs or increase speed. At comScore, we are continuously enhancing our products and developing new ones. We think it's important to introduce new products/features as quickly as possible, so as to gain or maintain a competitive advantage.

If I'm stuck in a rut and can't resolve a problem, I discuss the problem with as many relevant people as possible to get ideas for a solution. I am very persistent and don't give up easily.

In terms of trying out our ideas on different target markets to see if they work, at comScore we tend to introduce a product broadly, then quickly gauge the reaction of different target segments within the broad market. Negative reaction makes me sit back and re-examine the product, the value it provides to customers, and our approach to selling and marketing. I don't give up easily, but in today's fast-moving business world one doesn't have a lot of time to get it right.

At comScore, we have a culture of innovation and we try to patent our ideas as much as we can. However we have had instances of competitors copying our ideas. It spurs us on to continuously innovate.

comScore is a public company and strong growth in revenue and profit is expected by our shareholders. We strive to provide it. It's the reality of life as a high-tech public company.

Being first to market is a huge advantage, but one has to be careful to not be first with an inferior product that competitors can then leapfrog with a higher quality product of their own. Balancing speed with reliability and quality is vital and not always easy to do. On the rare occasions where a competitor introduces a product that's superior to one of ours, we innovate rapidly and try to leapfrog the competitor with advantages that we can uniquely provide.

I find it difficult to switch off from work mode. I typically work five full-time and two part-time days a week for a total of 60+ hours per week, although I do try to take days/weekends off here and there. Today, with electronic communication, it's easy to take time off while still staying in touch with business.

I do like to 'work hard, play hard' and can be obsessive about things when they mean a lot to me. However, I don't think I've ever suffered consequences from family and friends. I always seem to be able to skate by somehow. My wife and I have chosen not to have children, but if we did I would have to work harder at balancing my work and personal life."

The situations that cause me the most stress at work include:

- Having to meet quarterly financial targets as a public company.
- Deadlines.
- Difficult clients.
- Losing a valuable employee.
- Data issues.
- Technology changing at an ever-increasing pace.
- Surprising enhancements to competitors' products.

The advice I'd give to people who find it difficult to cope with stress at work and at home is to start a daily exercise regimen and try to get a solid seven to eight hours of sleep per night.

The qualities I look for from employees:

- People who have strong quantitative and communication skills.
- People who are curious and self-starters.
- People who dislike the status quo and who are interested in changing things.

- People who are motivated to succeed and who work hard.
- For the appropriate positions, people who are good managers.

However, it is extremely rare to find all of these traits in the same person. I've often found that good managers don't make good leaders or innovators. And, many good COOs don't make very good CEOs. There's a big difference between being a manager and being a leader.

If employees don't meet their targets, I believe in giving them an opportunity to improve, but the leash must be short. One simply doesn't have the time to delay personnel decisions for too long in today's business climate. But before termination I would carefully consider whether there is another more suitable position for the employee to remain at the company.

I am always accessible to staff and try to do my best to communicate clearly with them. I want them to feel they are 'on the inside looking out'. I also believe that clear and motivating communication is a trait of great leaders. But I try to never let my employees 'see me sweat'" I try to show a realistic positive and optimistic outlook at all times. I think that it's reassuring and motivating to employees – but it can't come across as Polyannish! Today at comScore, I am only occasionally involved with the hiring and the firing of staff. Fortunately, I've never been in the position of regretting firing someone who then went on to achieve success elsewhere, but I've certainly been in the position of wishing I had been able to retain some people who left voluntarily and who achieved success elsewhere. I definitely inject humor into the workplace when required to offset stress and to help make employees feel energized. Humor is a terrific stress reducer that's also effective in getting people focused, motivated and, working hard.

The most important thing I've learnt about business is that in building great companies nothing happens without a relentless desire to be successful, a great deal of hard work, a flexible strategic plan, and a top-notch team.

If I had to start all over, I would pursue the same career path but there are certainly many mistakes I made along the way in the past that my experience would help me avoid or correct the second time around."

ANALYSIS AND ADVICE

This interview highlights a number of important strategies to deal with the inevitable pressures of work. First, create a team around you that provides the social support you need to do your job, and who you can turn to when times get tough – as we have seen over the last seven years of the recession.

Second, ensure that communications at the top of the organization are open and honest, because many of the stresses that people experience at work are related to "not knowing" what is happening at the top or in the organization as a whole. This scenario usually leads to rumor spreading and uncertainty. As Ronald Reagan once humorously quipped: "I've always believed that a lot of the troubles in the world would disappear if we were talking to each other instead of about each other."

Third, the tensions that build up in the workplace or even in the home can frequently be relieved temporarily by humor, so that the underlying tensions can eventually be brought to the surface and dealt with. Humor not only relieves tension, but also creates an atmosphere where people, in a less than confrontational way, can talk more informally about their problems.

Fourth, being flexible appears again as a coping strategy that unlocks problems rather than exacerbates them.

And finally, having passion for what you do means that you and the people around you will enjoy the nine to five rather than tolerate it.

chapter 8

Debra A. Pruent – Chief Operating Officer, GfK Consumer Experiences

Debra Pruent is Chief Operating Officer of GfK Consumer Experiences and a member of the GfK SE Management Board. She is responsible for the company's global custom research business and plays a lead role in M&A activity for this sector, including GfK's most recent acquisitions of Knowledge Networks and Bridgehead International.

She has significant experience in the market research industry. Prior to her current role, she was COO of GfK Custom Research North America and Chief Executive Officer of NOP World Automotive US, which was acquired by the GfK Group in 2005. In 1991, after ten years with General Motors, Debra joined automotive market researchers Allison-Fisher International (which later became a part of NOP World) as a partner.

Debra holds a BS in Mathematics and Computer Science from Wayne State University in Detroit, Michigan, and an MS in Applied Statistics from Oakland University in Rochester, Michigan, where she also lectured in the Department of Mathematics. Debra currently serves on the Advertising Research Foundation's Board of Directors and is actively involved in helping to shape the future of advertising research.

She has built up extensive M&A experience within the Market Research industry from a variety of perspectives throughout her career. This includes both actively selling a company (Allison-Fisher, bought by UBM) and being acquired (as part of NOP World, acquired by GfK). In addition, since becoming part of GfK in 2005, Debra has had a hands-on leadership role for multiple integrations in the US and, since 2008, Management Board-level responsibility for the strategic screening, negotiation and purchase of companies to complement GfK's global portfolio.

About Debra

"I am the oldest of six children (we were born close together) and I am very close to my family. I've been told that I was born 'a little old lady' and my parents have always remarked on how driven I am. They spent most of my childhood trying to get me to relax and not to push myself so hard. I cried if I missed a day of school and can remember begging my dad to go to my school to get my homework when I was sick with chickenpox. He said: 'but you're only in the 3rd grade – what are you missing?' He eventually gave in and went to my school to collect the homework. My brothers and sisters, while good students, didn't have these characteristics, which my parents found strange. I have always worked hard to be good in school and generally, but wouldn't consider myself to be a perfectionist. I have a 'work hard' gene and seem to have been born with it.

My Grade 8 Algebra teacher was instrumental in shaping my career. The love she gave me for math created a 'mission' from the age of 12 to pursue mathematics as my university major. I received degrees in Mathematics and Computer Science and started at General Motors after university (I had two different roles within my nine years there) and was then recruited by a relatively new company who were focused on automotive market research. After ten years, the company was acquired to become part of a larger market research company, then sold to GfK in 2005, which is where I work today. I became a Management Board member in 2008.

I firmly believe that the six key points in business are:

1. Understanding how your business makes money.
2. Having a good strategy and understanding how you will differentiate and/or excel in your market.

3. Hiring the right people.
4. Clear and constant communication within the organization.
5. Executional discipline.
6. Regular feedback loops – what's going right and wrong – and creating a 'learning organizational' culture.

I also think that the other key points in being successful in business are: a strong work ethic, social intelligence, learning agility, strong ethical morals, ability to handle stress, and the ability to have fun!

I have definitely learnt from successes and failures, particularly failures. In the global business that I run, there are constant setbacks and successes as part of managing a large and diverse portfolio of companies. One of the larger global setbacks was the economic crisis of 2009, in which we had a very significant revenue decline but were not able to quickly adapt with respect to our variable costs (mostly people). We were able to 'bounce back' through a very thorough understanding of the circumstances under which we got caught. This was followed by a lot of honest communication and commitment to put things in place to prevent this happening in the future. This is the common cycle of setbacks as I know it and requires a commitment to being an agile, learning organization.

My best (personal) business investment was becoming a shareholder in the second company I worked for. This allowed me to take ownership and accountability for all aspects of the business, which is difficult if not impossible to do if you work for a public company. In my opinion, even with the best intentions and compensation tied to performance, if the money isn't yours in the first place, it is impossible to feel the same level of responsibility or accountability. My worst business investment was the acquisition of a company whose culture, driven by its owner, was at odds with our company. Integrating was not only impossible, but the company itself caused additional problems in the region which also had to be dealt with. This taught me to be very skeptical of acquiring 'people companies' and to pay more attention to culture if the acquisition is necessary.

I take risks in business that are mostly to do with trusting the passion (and knowledge if it is an area outside of my specific competency, but salient to the overall business) of someone else's investment plan for a project, new acquisition, or product. I only make 'gut decisions' in areas where I have at least 15 years of experience; otherwise all my decisions are based on hard facts.

My biggest company success to date was the successful implementation of a new strategy that involved significant management board changes, as well as several organizational and senior management changes. During this time, our overall employee engagement went up two years in a row and the positive energy (and results) in the company were beyond our expectations.

I am careful not to overspend and very conscious of cost control. I don't have a philosophy of 'spreading investment'. I take each opportunity as it comes and make my decisions based on the current environment. I am open to both low and higher risk investments as long as they are well thought out and have measurement plans, including conditions to 'stop' in place.

I regularly make priority lists and almost always have a 'what do I need to accomplish today' list, as well as ongoing 'To Do' lists. However, I have come to accept over many years that, due to 'unexpected priorities', I often only have one or two things crossed off my 'today' list at the end of the day!

I am constantly making modifications to my business (go-to-market execution, product updates, business processes, and how we work internally) while staying true to the overall strategy. I feel that I am always learning something new about our market, the business environment, our competition, how we execute internally, etc. and that influences my desire to implement change. Process changes are always, at least by me, considered initially in a 'test mode' and usually run within one country, region, or appropriate sub-organization to make sure they make sense.

If I can't resolve a business problem, I usually set up a 'brainstorming' session. I believe 100% in the adage that the more smart people you get together in a room, the more likely you are to resolve a problem. I like to talk through the issues with trusted advisors, or a small group. I often have 'brilliant moments' when my brain has been stimulated by these sessions but is 'off'/'relaxed' while I am falling asleep or taking a shower. I have resolved many problems this way!

I try out my ideas on different target markets. This is often the case within the product development side of our business. We discuss and run 'pilot projects' with specific target groups (e.g. certain clients) to improve our chances of broader success. I wouldn't say that negative reaction has made us more determined to succeed, but it has definitely helped to sharpen some aspects of our ideas.

I definitely believe in teamwork. Every business needs to have scale and that can't come from a single 'Great Man' model. Many different skill sets are needed to keep a business successful and thriving, and the collaboration that comes from good partnerships is also a source of the energy needed to run a business.

I am constantly raising the bar for hitting bigger targets and growing the business, which I realize can cause stress on the broader organization. I believe that pushing people to achieve something they didn't think they could can bring huge satisfaction and reward. However, not everyone is 'up' for such a journey and when you raise the bar but can't achieve it in a given year it can be a huge deflator to the organization. So I'm conscious that I need to find the balance, which I work on constantly.

Timing is absolutely crucial in business in launching a new idea or service. A business unit of our company is focused on helping companies innovate in their markets and we have a myriad of examples of the 'right product at the wrong time' (and how to navigate this). Our company is currently in the midst of launching something that is 'the future' (in our opinion!), but that may be at the wrong time with respect to a natural resistance to let go of the present approach, even when everyone agrees that it is substandard. The will of companies not to change, even when they know it is inevitable, is huge and in these cases it can take a combination of strong communication, a fearless market leader, and perhaps some negative consequences of the current approach to implement change. Otherwise one must wait for the more natural evolution, which is slow and sub-efficient in the market.

I work, on average, about 70 hours a week. I don't find it difficult to transition to 'non-work' activities at all; however, I'm mainly in work mode. I don't consider myself as a 'play hard' person, at least not on a regular basis, and enjoy going out, or travelling with friends or family. Because I travel quite a bit for work, I sometimes feel that I am missing out on time with family and friends; however, they often have even less free time than me!

How do you deal with stress?

When it comes to dealing with stress, I don't have a particular strategy, other than I tend to talk a lot. Instead of shutting down, or becoming isolated or depressed, I become more talkative. I also work longer hours and get into a highly 'multi-tasking' mode. I tend to sleep less but I'm not tired. I like to do some physical activity if I'm stressed, such as walking and cycling; however, I rarely have time to do any exercise, so I wouldn't consider them as part of my 'coping strategy'. I try to end each day with a hot bath to reflect and let myself connect dots and, hopefully) have 'Aha!' moments.

I have never had a nervous breakdown, or lost the ability to cope; however, I have come close. I had a period of 'panic attacks' in the middle of my career which had to be temporarily managed with medication and I saw a psychologist who helped me to cope. Thankfully, I fully recovered and actually felt myself stronger than ever with respect to coping after this episode.

The situations that cause me the most stress at work are deadlines and difficult people; as well as a negative outcome on the overall (e.g. business unit or company) performance within some areas of my responsibility. Another thing that causes me stress is not being in control or on top of something. My advice if you suffer with stress is to confront the issues (e.g. work through to finish a report; call a client who is upset; confront a co-worker on an issue, etc.). Accept that most things aren't perfect and that very few jobs are influencing life and death. Work through the hard tasks, do your best and let go of the outcomes.

The qualities I look for from my employees are a strong work ethic and high level of personal responsibility, combined with good intelligence and a willingness to learn. When it comes to 'target achievement' I respect effort as much as results and can accept lack of target achievement if we have learnt something which helps us in the future.

I am always accessible to employees. My assistant says I am 'too accessible compared to the average executive. This can be positive or negative, depending on which way you look at it.

I am involved with hiring and firing of staff and have helped people who I have 'fired' to find positions which fit their skills and comfort level elsewhere.

I believe in injecting humor into the workplace. For example, I always remind people in my company that we are 'not curing cancer'. No one dies if our market research project is behind schedule or doesn't produce the expected results for clients. In other words, let's always put our stress in perspective!

My advice to aspiring business entrepreneurs: strategy is important, but execution is everything. You need to execute and complete stages of your business plan before going on to the next stage or you will soon find yourself with a business where every aspect is a 'critical ball in the air.

The most important thing I have learnt about business is that finding the right people makes all the difference. I heard a saying many years ago that's 100% true – 'culture eats strategy for lunch'. So if you don't have the right people on board you are spending way too much energy trying to point people in the right direction, instead of moving the business forward. I completely understand that not everyone understands or accepts a company's strategy or culture, but then we need to strongly encourage them to 'vote with their feet'."

ANALYSIS AND ADVICE

There are a number of "take home" points raised in this interview. The first is that learning to deal with difficult people is a priority for highly pressured people. The "glass half empty" people, or pessimists, are difficult to manage, and cause most of us trouble in the work environment. This means selecting the most socially and interpersonally skilled people, and giving constructive feedback to those who are nay-sayers and "can't do that, we tried it before and it didn't work" types – to develop them to be more positive.

Second, prioritize your workload and ensure that deadlines are realistic and achievable. With business moving at such a pace, it is important to ensure that your workload is manageable, deadlines realistic, and objectives clear and communicated.

Third, the issue of control comes up again – that is, taking control of events rather than letting them overwhelm you – which means not necessarily relying on others to sort out your problems but taking ownership yourself. We like the idea of "emotionally off-loading," finding people in the work environment you can "let off steam" with. By externalizing your worries to others, they can help you find solutions before the problem becomes either serious or very serious.

Fourth, again we are hearing from our interviewees that humor is essential for bonding, reducing the tension, and allowing people to unwrap the underlying problem so that a solution can be found.

Fifth, there is a need from time to time to relax and unwind, expressed by many who work in high-pressure jobs. Leonardo da Vinci once wrote: "every now and then go away and have a little relaxation. To remain constantly at work will diminish our judgement. Go some distance away, because work will be in perspective and a lack of harmony is more readily seen." And finally, the notion that "culture eats strategy for lunch" is quite significant, and implying how we treat one another and work together is more important than "the vision statement."

chapter 9

Gale D. Metzger – Former Co-Founder and President, Statistical Research Inc. (SRI)

Gale Metzger has served as Chairman of the Advertising Research Foundation's (ARF) Board of Directors, and as Chairman of its Research Quality Council. He is a former president of the Market Research Council and of the Radio and Television Research Council. The Market Research Council has inducted Gale into its Hall of Fame and the National Association of Broadcasters gave him the Hugh Malcolm Beville award in recognition of his distinguished professional career in broadcast audience research. In 2009, the ARF presented its Lifetime Achievement Award to Gale for his outstanding service to the industry.

He has authored papers on statistical topics, including sampling and survey research procedures. The firm played a key role in the development of Computer-Assisted Telephone Interviewing (CATI) and Random Digit Dialing (RDD) – both breakthroughs that enabled significant improvements in research quality.

Gale's 50-year career in the business nexus has made him a close witness to US media research history. In 2005, he provided an overview of TV audience measurement to an industry meeting on accountability of measurement services. He testified before the Senate Committee on Commerce, Science, and Technology concerning proposed legislation, the FAIR Ratings Act of 2005 (S.1372).

Born in Dayton, Ohio, Gale received his BA from Northwestern University, where he did graduate work. He began his career at AC Nielsen in 1958 and founded Statistical Research in 1968 with Gerald Glasser. The SRI RADAR service was sold in 2001 to ARBITRON and the other SRI services were sold to Knowledge Networks, Inc. in the same year. He served as a consultant to GfK/Knowledge Networks/SRI and others.

About Gale

"I was brought up in an extended farm family in Ohio. My parents were very industrious, with a strong work ethic. We were all expected to do family farm duties and there were no exceptions for age or gender.

My parents were working class. They grew up in the 1920s and 30s, yielding a depression mentality.

I never thought of myself as 'hard up' even though there was no extra money around. My motivation was to provide for my family, to do work that was challenging and interesting, and contribute to society. At the end of one summer's employment on a factory production line, the plant supervisor spoke to me about my future. He articulated the hope that after my schooling was complete I would return for permanent employment opportunities. Having experienced mind-numbing assembly line work, my unspoken thought was that my mission in college was to avoid having to do that type of work to earn a living.

I did well at school. I was the first in my family to go to college. I had a full scholarship and covered costs through part-time jobs. Finding a real job was a fluke; advancement in the job was based on my good educational background, training, and initiative.

My parents also taught me humility, which translated to good management skills. No matter what the task, legitimate work is self-redeeming. I think that you should never think of yourself as too good for any job. Do not ask anything of someone else that you wouldn't do yourself. Acting out that philosophy and 'pitching in' was a good leadership skill.

I worked steadily from the age of ten in a variety of menial jobs from delivering newspapers, cleaning, and delivery tasks to apprentice plumber, factory assembly line, painting airport runway markings, etc. Professionally I made steady advancement from clerk to management of statistical methods to general management with the AC Nielsen company. After ten years, I elected with a partner to start our own company.

I knew I was good at and enjoyed math and statistics. My career was consistent with those skills, but resulted from a series of fortuitous occurrences and good performance on the job. My management abilities intermixed well with my technical competence and enabled my advancement. My goal was always to deliver more than was expected in less time than expected – which earned more opportunities. The company that we formed, Statistical Research Inc., provided market and media research information to major media companies and advertisers. We provided the national radio audiences in the US from 1972 until 2000.

How do you deal with stress?

Stress is part of life! The key is to act promptly to avoid a build-up. All associates know that problems and errors occur. They also know to report problems to management for a positive resolution. If a client is involved, they are notified immediately after options to resolve are defined and action is taken in counsel with the client.

My strategies for dealing with stress: (1) Exercise each morning – it clears the mind. (2) Discuss any issues with personal and business partners. They include my wife, business partner, lawyer, accountant, and clients. (3) Deal with issues promptly and work to avoid build-up."

What are the main challenges you have faced?

"Early in my career, a Nielsen crisis involved me mobilizing a crew of people, travelling many hours to an off-site location, and hand-tabulating results from a major survey for delivery of results to the Board Chairman and major clients the next day. It was an all-nighter for the team. A rapport was built and all exulted in the benefits achieved for the company. It was an excellent model for future endeavors. Mission impossible became possible. Relationships forged under pressure served all well and that experience facilitated other efforts in the years that followed.

Late in my career, our company was asked to build a television audience measurement system (SMART – Systems for Measuring and Reporting Television) to compete with Nielsen – $50,000,000 budget over ten years. To accomplish the task, a new team was created from existing personnel and new hires. It involved an extension of existing activities and new endeavors. For example, we hired engineers and got into manufacturing engineering hardware. We designed and manufactured television-metering devices and installed them in a sample of homes in a Philadelphia laboratory. We created a data reporting system that put survey results on client desktop computers for next day access. The industry participated directly through special committees that were motivated by client management directives. The linkage with the client community was strengthened by the steady interactions. The spillover from this assignment also led to other opportunities associated with our core business.

I think that the key to finding time to oversee and manage various aspects of work is to work diligently, hire well, and delegate. We had a great team of intelligent, hard-working colleagues and great client relationships, which all helped.

My tips for being successful in business are:

1. Select an arena that is dynamic and growing and where your skills facilitate solutions to known needs.
2. Work diligently.
3. Hire smart people with strong work ethics.
4. Foster close and trusting relationships with associates and clients through top performance.
5. Operate openly and fairly with bold integrity.
6. Face problems quickly and cleanly – do not allow them to fester.
7. Make every decision as if it were to be front page news.

8. Never surprise a client with negative news – keep clients abreast of developing situations and involve them as part of the solution.
9. Keep up with what's new, particularly technology that facilitates more efficient business practices.

My biggest setback in business was the failure of the industry to fund the SMART national rollout. Because that possibility had been anticipated, a shutdown fund was included in the contract. As a result, there was less adverse financial effect than there would have been without that foresight. All terminated employees were given reasoned separation packages and assisted in finding other employment – all 'landed on their feet'. The company reverted to our ongoing 'normal' business. As a result, a 30-year record of steady growth was interrupted.

We started a new company after consultations with potential clients and after being assured that we would be given work opportunities. Potential client executives wrote open letters to financial institutions affirming that fact and to enable me to acquire a home mortgage. On an ongoing basis, we minimized risks by assuring business levels before investing in people or equipment. Gut instinct, on its own, was never enough.

My biggest business success to date was building a successful business and gainfully employing a professional staff of 30 plus approximately 100 additional full-time associates; creating and running a profitable business that grew in gross revenues year after year for 30 years up until the SMART laboratory was shut down.

As a privately owned entity, we were less pressured by outside influences and responded to market needs. Services were launched only after assurances of sufficient revenues to cover out-of-pocket costs – with the knowledge that if we had that much advance support, more would arise with a real product in hand. I discount my own 'beliefs' and rely instead on latent, demonstrated needs. If potential clients do not perceive a need, what I think does not matter. I was never successful at creating a demand for a service unless there was a pre-existing need.

My target was always to create better services. We never acted only to increase revenues. If we produced a valued service on a timely basis, the revenue always followed. We turned down 'opportunities' that were out-side our expertise, or that were simply 'work for hire' that effectively could have been done by anyone. The work we did should in some way extend our service portfolio. For example, AT&T urged us to operate a telephone call centre to be operated to their specifications for a defined profit. While that would have increased our volume and profit, we politely declined because we saw it as a diversion from doing more creative work.

My advice to people who find it difficult to cope with stress at work is:

1. Live a multi-faceted life. Find challenging diversions – arts, or entertain-ment, or education. Life should be a multi-legged stool and if someone kicks out one leg, the stool remains standing on the remaining supports.
2. Live a life of integrity and candor.
3. Address the cause of the stress and diffuse before it builds up.

The qualities I look for from people who work for me are intelligence, aptitude, strong work ethic, reasonable social skills, and motivation. I've no regrets if I fired someone who went on to achieve success elsewhere. It's a win–win if that happens, as we are better off without them and they are better off in their new position.

My advice to enterprising businessmen and women who are keen to become successful in their career is:

1. Address a defined need. Do not attempt to generate business condi-tioned on creating a demand.
2. Do not incur costs without some defined basis to cover, including hiring new personnel.
3. Be assured of competence in the defined arena and a competitive edge over what already exists."

ANALYSIS AND ADVICE

This interview highlighted a number of strategies to deal with the stress of running a successful business. First, forging rela-tionships under pressure can be important in creating a social support group among working colleagues. Most people are working in organizations undergoing constant change, with heavier workloads, and impossible deadlines, but transforming pressure into a Dunkirk spirit – into team building and camaraderie – can make the journey to achieving objectives much easier and keep stress at bay.

Second, when problems do occur, it is vital to resolve them quickly, avoiding any build-up of stress. This is a lesson that many high-pressure executives understand, but because of their busy lives, frequently neglect to deal with in a timely fashion.

Third, be humble in your relationships with people at work: "never think of yourself as too good for any job" is a mantra that should be practiced by senior people in management or in any other walk of life. Humility and a "down to earth" attitude to others will help to forge more meaningful relationships and a culture of trust, where the pressures of work can be surfaced and dealt with quickly.

Fourth is the issue of finding "challenging diversions," being engaged in activities outside of business or your main preoccupation. To put the pressures of a job into context, it is always worthwhile to have a passion outside of work, whether in the arts, sports, education, or a specific hobby. As Vincent van Gogh once wrote "I put my heart and soul into my work, and lost my mind in the process." And finally, "be a real person," try to relate to people not from your role but from the core of who you are.

chapter 10

Jack Kraft – Former Vice-Chairman and COO, Leo Burnett Advertising Agency

Jack Kraft has more than 35 years of diversified top management experience. Originally, he was in the advertising and marketing business with two of the top companies in the field. For the past 15 years Jack has been an active Founder, Investor, Adviser, and/or Board Member of a number of firms with an emphasis on technology-related service firms.

He retired as Vice-Chairman, COO of the Leo Burnett Company, a leading multi-national advertising agency, in 1992 after nearly 20 years. At retirement he was a member of the Executive Committee, a Board member and Chair of the Finance Committee. During 1993–94, he joined Young and Rubicam as EVP/Chief Administrative Officer and member of the Board. Jack has participated in the development of a number Internet-related firms. Among them, Modem Media, a pioneering Interactive Ad Agency that went public, was acquired by Digitas as is now part of Publicis Group.

He was a founder of Two-Way Communications, a similar company, which was sold to iXL, went public, became part of Avenue A/Razorfish/aQuantive and was acquired by Microsoft. It is now part of Publicis.

After investing in and joining the BOD of Lante Corporation, which completed an IPO in 2000, Jack became Chairman and managed the sale of the firm to SBI, which ultimately was consolidated into Avenue A/Razorfish/aQuantive/Microsoft and now Publicis.

Jack regularly consults with a wide range of developing companies on matters of structure, growth, management development, and corporate opportunities. Recently, Jack served on the Board of APAC Customer Services Inc. (NASDAQ, APAC), ConsumerBase, a behavioral data company. He's also an Adviser to RISE INTERACTIVE.COM, an Internet marketing firm, and is a Senior Advisor at The Chicago Corporation, an Investment Banking firm.

Jack is a member of the Chicago Central Area Committee (CCAC) and The Economic Club of Chicago. He is also active at the Entrepreneurship & Innovation program at the Kellogg Graduate School judging business plans and mentoring students.

About Jack

"There are two areas from early childhood that were definitely formative:

1. Growing up during World War II, I was effectively raised by women as all the men were away. I saw women doing everything, so I was never burdened by pre-conceived gender roles, which later positively affected my career.
2. At the age of six an injury cost me the sight of my right eye. I was perceived as 'handicapped' and attended a 'special' school. That experience taught me to appreciate what people can do – not what they can't – and that was a significant lesson.

My parents were working class, but had some entrepreneurial success to reach middle class status.

I have experienced hard times and lack of money. When I was 22, I had three children, was working in two jobs, and going to night school. Having to feed a family is a powerful motivation to succeed in life.

I was academic, which was key to landing my first job. The combination of academics and practical experience became the basis for a career.

I worked in a variety of jobs in the early days, including the original McDonald's restaurant in Des Plaines, Illinois, then as a clerk, bookkeeper, accountant, auditor, personal assistant, and junior manager.

The worst pressures for me are decisions related to people: staff selection, development, promotion, and termination. Other pressures are related to acquisition of other businesses and their integration.

I generally find time to oversee and manage the various aspects of the work by being organized and working long hours. Like most people in business, I get stressed, but try to use it to stay focused. I've learnt to work around things that I can't change.

The key points for being successful in business: differentiation, relevance, familiarity, control, superb staff, and paranoia.

My biggest setback in business was trying to develop a business incubator and finding that small businesses are more difficult to manage than bigger ones. We quickly 'triaged' the portfolio using IP, industry insights, and talent to create and offer services – sometimes to competitors.

When it comes to making decisions, I feel that decisions based on fact are usually not risky. Decisions based on gut instinct are usually always risky.

My biggest business success to date was participating in the establishment of Leo Burnett as a multi-national agency, and more recently leading a management change that turned around a public outsourcing company.

I have no problem overspending a budget that is driving successful results. Depending on the circumstances, spreading investments solely to mitigate risk can assure failure by underfunding them all.

I don't like change unless it's absolutely necessary. Change for change's sake wears people out. Innovation, on the other hand is essential for all constituencies, customers, staff, and investors. I love ideas!

My views on problem solving: brainstorming in groups is stimulating, if properly led. Enforce the rule that, initially, 'there are no bad ideas', so that all possibilities are considered. The least senior staff should speak first. No one should be allowed to criticize another idea until all have spoken. And no one who doesn't have an idea should be allowed to criticize at all.

I believe in trying out ideas on different target markets to see if they work. A negative reaction is a warning. Ignore it at your peril!

Raising the bar for hitting bigger targets is an art rooted in metrics. As a manager you need to be able to convince people why the bar is being raised and how and why it can be achieved.

Timing in business is only crucial if you're too late. Many first movers get trampled, with a lot of pioneers dying on the frontiers. My businesses have typically been refined versions of what's already out there.

How do you deal with stress?

The situations that cause me the most stress at work include difficult people, customers, staff, and investors.

My advice to people who find it difficult to cope with stress is to understand what's important.

A lot of things we worry about aren't important. Focus on what you can do something about. The rest is going to happen anyway. Realize that, ultimately, only people count. Everything else can be bought or replaced.

The qualities I look for from people who work for me include leadership, diligence, mental agility, pertinent business skills, manners, and personal presentation.

My advice to enterprising businessmen and women: be prepared to compete. If you're not competitive, success will be limited. Excellence attracts money. Employers hire on promise, but only reward on performance. Your best chance for success is to be first in and last out of the office. It's the first thing employers notice.

The most important lessons I've learnt about business:

- The harder I work, the luckier I get.
- Try to stay close to the best people, both bosses and peers.
- Quality people in your life will demonstrate success and most will help you achieve it.

I was slow to realize the importance of relationships to success. If I started from scratch, I would invest more in relationships – professionally, personally, and with family."

ANALYSIS AND ADVICE

This interview raises several very important questions about the quality of working lives. First and foremost is the importance of the people you work with for your success, and as a barrier to suffering too much stress.

Second, many senior people in business introduce "change for change's sake," not appreciating that constant change is a major stressor for many people in the workplace.

Third, successful people (we have observed throughout this book) admit to being impatient and quick-tempered, and making decisions too quickly. The consequences of these decisions can cause excessive pressure, so it is better to have other people around you who can get you to reflect, for a short time, on an important decision. Invariably, successful people are more Type A as opposed to Type B personalities, that is, ambitious, fast moving, assertive, decisive, rushed, and impatient. But research shows that Type A personality types have a significantly higher risk of heart disease and other stress-related illnesses than Type Bs, who are more laid back, less rushed, and less ambitious. Controlling Type A behavior is important: you may never change a Type A person into a B but modifying this behavior is possible.

Fourth, and repeated again here, is that one should focus on doing "what you can do something about" and not on things you can't change.

It is interesting to note, once again, that many of the successful people we interviewed came from working class backgrounds, or had some adverse life events early in their life, with a driver to do better and gain some control over the world that they didn't have in their youth – not the desire for power but for personal control.

chapter 11

Joan Chow – Executive Vice President and Chief Marketing Officer, ConAgra Foods

Joan joined ConAgra Foods as Executive Vice President and Chief Marketing Officer in 2007. In this role, she is responsible for leading ConAgra Foods' global marketing team, including integrated marketing planning, digital/ interactive marketing, advertising, social media, consumer insights, and multicultural marketing.

One of Brandweek's *2009 Marketers of the Year, Joan takes an in-depth focus on insights-driven marketing for ConAgra Foods' brands across the portfolio. Joan strives to build integrated 360-degree marketing programs, including compelling advertising, creative, effective media plans, sustainable customer/shopper linkage, and a strong return on marketing objectives.*

Joan's marketing organization and the ConAgra Foods Foundation partnered on the company's cause marketing effort – Child Hunger Ends Here – focused on ConAgra Foods' longstanding commitment to ending child hunger in America. Joan and her team also launched www.ReadySetEat.com, a unique website that not only offers quick, easy recipes for dinners and desserts, but also highlights the ingredients that are on sale at local grocers.

Prior to joining ConAgra Foods, Joan was senior vice president and chief marketing officer of Sears, Roebuck & Co., where she led all aspects of the company's retail marketing efforts. Prior to joining Sears in 1998, she spent seven years at Information Resources, Inc. She began her career in 1986 at Johnson & Johnson Consumer Products, Inc.

Joan serves as a member on the Board of Directors of Feeding America, Association of National Advertisers (ANA) and The Manitowoc Company, Inc., and has previously served on the Board of RC2 Corporation. She earned her MBA from The Wharton School of the University of Pennsylvania and her bachelor's degree in linguistics from Cornell University.

About Joan

"My father was a diplomat for Taiwan, and his speciality was Central and Latin America. As a result, my sister, brother, and I (I'm the youngest) were all born in Central American countries. I was born in Cuba, then lived in Argentina, Taiwan, Brazil, and Spain. I came to the US when I was 13. I have a close relationship with my parents and siblings. My parents had high expectations for education and grades and always demanded that we compared ourselves to our potential, and not to others.

My parents were solid middle class. Diplomats for Taiwan were not paid well during the time my father worked. We were brought up knowing we didn't have much money, and they instilled a 'saver's' mentality in us. I think my parents were recycling before it became popular and green!

We weren't hard up but we didn't have extra money. For example, I wanted to join the Girl Scouts but we couldn't afford to pay the fees. So I was very motivated to save money and also knew what I could live with and live without. All I was focused on was getting a very good education. Success was defined as getting a good education; it was not about getting a good job or making a lot of money.

I studied hard and got good grades. The biggest impact on me finding a job was getting my MBA at The Wharton School. I majored in linguistics when I was at Cornell University for my undergraduate degree. And given my family's emphasis on getting an education, no one coached me on the need to get a job upon graduation. No one in our family worked in business – they were mostly doctors and government employees. I remember signing up for interviews when I was a senior because everyone else was doing that, and I was completely unprepared for the interviews and knew nothing about the companies. As a result, I didn't get a job when I graduated and moved back home. I pounded the pavement and got a job as an administrative assistant at Ernst & Whinney in their utility consulting group. I was fortunate to work for a partner who saw a lot of potential in me; he encouraged me to get my MBA, and that is how I ended up at Wharton.

Wharton was my launching pad. Many companies came to recruit at Wharton, and I was drawn to the packaged goods companies and realized that my passion was brand management. I joined Johnson & Johnson upon graduation and spent five years there.

After my five years at J&J, I realized that I was very analytically oriented, and I joined IRI (a marketing information and analytics firm). I was there for seven years until I started reading about customer relationship marketing, and I joined Sears, Roebuck & Company's Home Services division to form their CRM department. I ended up staying at Sears for nine years – eventually being promoted to Chief Marketing Officer for Sears Retail. Now I'm at ConAgra Foods as EVP/Chief Marketing Officer (close to six years), so I'd say I've come full circle to being back in packaged goods marketing. I realized when I joined Sears that my love is marketing, not general management.

I would say the key points in being successful in business are: **Ask**, **Sell**, **Tell**: Ask is about curiosity; seeking to understand other people's points of view; getting feedback; and not being too proud to ask for help when needed. Sell is about influencing others; having conviction about your ideas; and getting people to buy-in. Tell is telling stories about your consumers/customers so people can understand their needs/wants; informing people about your expectations of their performance; and telling a compelling story about your ideas.

I learn more from failures than I do from successes. I've had marketing plans that didn't deliver the planned objectives. The root causes are typically that we didn't dig deep enough to get actionable insights or we assumed best case circumstances rather than reality. Marketers tend to be resilient. I'm focused on lessons learnt, and I definitely don't want to repeat the same mistake twice! Every year I hold lessons learnt sessions with my team, and one of them is always based on a failure.

Marketing is a balance of insights, data, and judgment. I was brought in at ConAgra Foods to build a centralized marketing function. At the time, the CEO had the vision, but many others in the brand organization felt that we were taking away a key responsibility of theirs. I think the following quote sums it up best – it was an orientation meeting I had with one of the general managers when I joined the company. 'I don't understand why we need a CMO. I've been a marketer my whole life, and everyone on my team is a marketer.' I would say that if you were to ask people now whether our marketing capabilities have been upgraded and whether there's 'demand' for marketing, people would tell you yes. And if you were to ask people whether ConAgra Foods is doing better marketing now, they'd say yes as well. We are careful about where we invest our dollars and people resources since we have many brands to support.

I'm not someone who puts together a 'To Do' list. My calendar is booked pretty much every day. I know my priorities for the quarter/month – I trust my team to know their daily priorities. If something unexpected comes up, I flex with it. I work closely with my administrative assistant so she knows which meetings are movable and which ones aren't.

I don't implement work changes for the sake of change. I will reorganize my team as the marketing world changes. For example, six years ago no one was talking about social media. Now we have a social media team and community managers.

Sometimes I will call a group together to help me through a problem. I don't think 'thinking time' can be scheduled. If there is a problem it's always processing somewhere in the back of my head. I use my commuting time and any time away from meetings to think.

We typically do a lot of research to figure out our target market. We test things both via research and in live test markets. Just because something didn't work the first time doesn't mean it's a bad idea. Refer back to the lessons learnt comment.

I believe in partnerships as I don't see how anyone can do anything in business by themselves. I am constantly raising the bar for hitting bigger targets and growing the business, and think that timing is crucial in launching a new idea or service, although the economy has put a damper on some new product launches.

I don't think I ever switch off completely from work mode. And being a marketer, I enjoy observing people and their shopping habits even in my spare time. That doesn't mean I can't relax and enjoy the weekends. I'm a hard worker, but not a workaholic. Occasionally I go through spurts of a lot of travel and time away from home, but it has not impacted on my family or friends."

How do you cope with stress?

"I exercise regularly. I love to read fiction and magazines, do crossword puzzles, and watch television. And I hug my husband – he's a wonderful stress reliever because he makes me laugh.

Situations at work that cause me the most stress are people who have points of view that are not substantiated by facts – 'anecdotal shrapnel' is a term I heard someone use that describes it. I like business problems – it's what I thrive on. People issues are more difficult.

My advice to people who find it difficult to cope with stress is to exercise and take walks. Get a dog.

In employees I look for people who don't accept the status quo and are willing to champion new ideas. I have regular conversations with my direct reports and always give them feedback on performance. I also arrange for some of them to have mentors in the company if that's helpful, and everyone knows where they stand with me.

I got some feedback a few years ago from my employees that I wasn't accessible (always in meetings). So I asked for feedback as to what the team would like. As a result of that feedback, I try to block every Friday morning to have breakfast in the cafeteria from 8–8:30 a.m. Anyone is welcome to join me. Sometimes I have four people, and other times I have 20. I also block time on my calendar to do 'Chow Time'. Up to five to six people at a time can sign up to join me in my office, eat popcorn, and talk about whatever they want. I also try to walk the halls and visit people in their offices as much as I can.

I inject humor into the workplace when required. My direct reports are all stand-up comedians in disguise. People often ask me what we do at my staff meetings, because all they hear is a lot of laughter. If I didn't have humor at work, I'd die. Besides, smile lines are more attractive than frown lines as you age.

The most important lesson I've learnt about business is that's it's about people. Once you figure the people out and what makes them tick, then you've done most of the hard work. Every business decision is inherently emotional – dig deep to figure out that emotion."

ANALYSIS AND ADVICE

We like the concept of "dig deep to figure out emotion" as a learning goal. Most of what happens in the workplace has an emotional component, and understanding decisions and change in this context might help to prevent stress and enhance more effective performance.

A second point raised in this interview is "understanding other people's point of view." Successful people frequently think they have the answers and don't turn on "receiver mode," but rather are on "transmit mode." As the social scientist Margaret Miller once commented "most conversations are simply monologues delivered in the presence of witnesses." So listening to others may help to understand what is really going on and to prevent many potential interpersonal conflicts, which can come from miscommunications.

Third, we all need to invest in our relationships outside of work, in our partners/spouses, children, close family, and friends as an important stress reliever, but also as a vehicle to test our actions with those who will be "critical friends," who will let you know what they truly think rather than give you the "socially desirable" response.

All of us also need an outlet for our feelings and emotions, which is best funneled through those who love and care about us. Sophocles wrote "one word frees us of all the weight and pain of life: that word is love." And finally, remember the power of humor, of the "arm around the shoulder," of the honestly spoken "thank you" and a smile.

Mark Conroy – Former President, Regent Seven Seas Cruises

Mark Conroy's former role at Regent Seven Seas Cruises was to oversee all day-to-day operations, marketing and sales, as well as to forecast revenue, profit goals, and company growth for Regent Seven Seas Cruises, the world's most inclusive, ultra-luxury cruise line. The award-winning brand is part of Prestige Cruise Holdings, which also owns Oceania Cruises.

A 40-year industry veteran, Mark joined the company as president and CEO of Diamond Cruises in 1992 and was instrumental in its merger with Seven Seas Cruise Line in 1995 to become Radisson Seven Seas Cruises, part of the Carlson group. In March 2006, Radisson aligned with sister brand Regent Hotels and Resorts and was renamed Regent Seven Seas Cruises. Mark served as president of both the hotel and cruise divisions until the company was acquired by Prestige in 2008.

Under his tenure, the line pioneered the all-balcony, all-suite concept, and launched the 700-guest Seven Seas Mariner (March 2001) and Seven Seas Voyager (April 2003), considered among the most luxurious ships afloat. The boutique, 480-guest Seven Seas Navigator (November 1999) completes the three-ship fleet.

One of the industry's most respected leaders, Mark previously served as president of both Renaissance Cruises and Commodore Cruise Line and as vice president of sales for Royal Viking Line. Over the years his expertise has been sought after and he often participates on executive-level panels. He was chairman of the Cruise Lines International Association from 2001 to 2004 and has served on various other industry committees.

Mark's introduction to the cruise industry was in 1973; working in the mailroom at Norwegian Cruise Line, while studying at the University of Miami, where he earned his bachelor's degree. He and his wife Marilyn have a daughter and live in Fort Lauderdale, Florida.

About Mark

"I was born in Iowa and was one of seven children. When I was six my father took a job where he had offices in Chicago and Milwaukee. He didn't want us to grow up in the cities so he and mom found a home in rural Wisconsin where the closest town (with 300 citizens) was three miles away. I was over 6 foot tall when I was 13 and when I began high school at 15 I reached my current height of 6′ 4″.

I was the Captain of the football team and also President of the student council for two years.

My father was a mechanical engineer and made a good living; however, he didn't have much left after taking care of his family. I always had plenty to eat, but if I wanted pocket money I had to earn it myself. We grew up in Wisconsin, where over half of the residents had second homes. From the time I was 11, I worked almost year round for a wealthy neighbor taking care of his property. He treated me quite well, which gave me a taste for the better things in life.

My parents lived through the depression and World War II. My father was a medic in the Pacific and all the death and destruction he saw impacted greatly on him. He was a functioning alcoholic for much of his adult life. When he drank, he became very difficult and I had to learn to cope for myself early in life. I was run over by a car at the age of four and spent almost a year in a body cast which forced me to stay in bed. As a result, I became an avid reader.

I have had a variety of jobs since I was 11. The wealthy neighbor I mentioned earlier taught me the basic skills of carpentry, construction, and even electrics, so during the summer I would do everything from mow his lawn, to paint his house, and keep his estate in good shape. At High School I worked in a ski resort to get free ski privileges. I started in the cafeteria, then worked in the restaurant as a cook, and eventually became a ski instructor. My best friend's dad ran a trucking company and got me a job in the summer and over the holiday period driving delivery trucks in Milwaukee. We were relief drivers, and each day we got to work never knowing where we were going to be assigned or what type of truck we would be driving. Most of the time it was delivering packages or furniture for a department store, and it taught me how to interact with all types of people and deal with all situations, including being robbed. The job paid well, but it was the most stressful job I ever had. While attending university, I worked part-time in a department store and was assigned to departments where someone failed to show up. My first job in the cruise industry was working weekends for NCL, helping people go through customs, including finding their bags, and filing damage baggage claims. During the afternoon I sold baggage insurance and gave out visitor passes.

I just fell into the job. Since I was doing well in school, I could pretty much set my own schedule. In the summer of 1973, when the trucking company I worked for in Milwaukee went on strike, I had no job to go to, and asked my boss at NCL if they could find me a full-time job in the office, which he did. The job required a certain amount of typing, which I was not very good at. I almost didn't get hired until I pointed out that if they modified their ticket layout they could use window envelopes and you didn't need to type to do the job. I was hired on the strength of this, but paid less because I couldn't type; however, I was allowed to work as much overtime as I wanted. Apart from my ticketing job, I worked in the mail room, delivered packages to the ship, met guests at the airport, and worked in accounts. I finally landed a full-time job in reservations, where I worked from 1:00 p.m. to 8:00 p.m. in the evening. I eventually became a supervisor in reservations and when I graduated from university I was offered a job in Corporate & Incentive Sales.

We ran a business that operated 365 days per year involving ships around the world. The ships are complicated, mechanical devices which have a crew of over 400 employees and from 500 to 700 guests each day. It's a complex business where things can and do go wrong. Fortunately, we hired a great team who reacted well to whatever situations they were faced with. In most cases, the problems we faced were external. They included airline delays, cancelled ports, excursions not working well, and even political problems. To make the business work you need to hire the right people and give them the tools and authority to do their job. When things go wrong you have to gather the facts, then be decisive, always keeping the guests' and crews' welfare in mind. As you make decisions, you have to think that if I was the guest or crew member, what I would think of the solution.

I joined the industry at the beginning, so there were there some great opportunities available. I think the hardest thing I faced at each company was the financial challenges, typically driven by outside forces beyond our control, such as war, recessions, acts of terror, revolutions, oil crisis, etc. Apart from this, we had financial challenges where the money was so tight we had to decide who got paid and who had to wait, and still concentrate on what we could do to turn things around and fill the ships at the right price. I found the best way to deal with this and all problems is to be open with all stakeholders and keep them informed.

My role changed while I was there and my focus was primarily to do with marketing, sales, and guest relations. That being said, the approach has not changed. You put the right people in the right job, give them proper direction, and let them and their staff get on with it. Then make sure you are measuring their success and giving them feedback accordingly. Delegation is important, and not something which I was particularly good at early on in my career.

We had a great team at Regent Seven Seas Cruises, great owners, and a pool of loyal guests who are very supportive. It always seemed we launched a ship during some sort of world crisis. The *Navigator* – Balkans War, the *Mariner* – 9/11, and the *Voyager* – the Gulf War. Each time we faced these challenges we put together a plan on how we were going to regain our momentum and we got all the stakeholders to buy into the plan. If they didn't, they typically would not stay with the company. We always worked at chunking down big problems into smaller, more manageable pieces which were easier for everyone to deal with. As we solved problems and changed course, we always kept our loyal guests, who ultimately pay our salaries, in mind.

My six key points in being successful in business are:

1. Build the right team.
2. Make a plan and execute it.
3. Stay focused.
4. Measure results and correct course.
5. Stay nimble and flexible and be decisive.
6. Stay humble and always run scared.

Setbacks in business are inevitable. I led the start-up of Renaissance Cruises for a Norwegian company and we did it only six months before the first ship was launched. The business got off to a good start, but due to the unrelated collapse and bankruptcy of our sponsor company we almost went under. My team and I had to get the parent company's banks to fund us to keep us alive until we could find a new buyer, which we did, allowing us to avoid bankruptcy. It was a successful failure.

My best investment was the time and effort I put into each of the jobs I did. The biggest mistake I made was not insisting on having a larger equity stake as part of my compensation in the companies I have run.

I take risks in business and base some of my decisions on gut instinct. I have been in the business since 1973 and have seen a lot of things work and fail. I think it is important to listen to your staff and your guests, then make the decision and hold yourself responsible for what happens afterwards. You undoubtedly learn from your mistakes.

My biggest business success to date (with the support of an excellent team) is seeing Regent Seven Seas Cruises grow from a single 350-guest ship cruise line to the most profitable and respected luxury cruise line in the world. I am now an advisor for them for the next two years.

When it comes to budgets, I always try to come up with a realistic budget and live within it. I learnt from the Chairman of RSSC that, if the ships are not full and there is business to be had, that it is acceptable to carefully overspend your marketing and sales budget to fill the ships. It is a highly fixed expense business with a perishable product. Once a cruise departs, the empty suites are lost until the next cruise. You can't save yourself rich!

My former role at RSSC was to focus on sales volume and guest satisfaction. They were the first things we addressed every day. When things went wrong, we assembled the necessary team to deal with the problem and made sure the rest of the team were focused on running the business and attaining our goals. You can't let problems allow you to take your eye off the ultimate goal.

Ships are self-contained and are successful in part because of the routines we developed and the highly consistent tasks that are performed each day. When we launched a new concept of services or food, we firstly tested it in the office, then in smaller groups aboard. When we had the proper results, we launched it fleet-wide. On the marketing and sales front, we tested offers or programs on selected departures over a limited time and if they were successful we rolled them out.

We tried to be proactive and not get stuck in a rut. Every week I had meetings with key team members to review what was going on and to address any new challenges. We tried to stay ahead of the rest of the market and develop new concepts, even though they may not have been needed at the time. New markets take a while to establish, so you need to be patient. We began by guerrilla marketing, by working with a few operators opportunistically. As the sales volume grew, we began working with a more strategic marketing plan and spent money. If they didn't work we changed directions as there's nothing to be gained from flogging a dead horse.

It's important to constantly raise the bar in order to hit bigger targets and grow the company. You either grow and prosper or eventually disappear. Our shareholders want a return on their investment and the only way we can do that is to improve our results and grow.

Timing is crucial in business. I remember launching one of the first cruises focusing on China just before the Tiananmen Square protests in 1989 happened. As a result, many guests cancelled. In 2012, we launched a series of cruises that began or ended in Egypt. They didn't sell well, so we decided to offer a special pre- and post-package, which worked well, despite all the bad news in the region. That being said, one of the beauties of our business is if something goes wrong in a region we can redeploy the assets to somewhere else.

The best example of good timing was the recession, which for us began in late 2008 when the stock market collapsed and bookings just stopped. In the past we had reacted to things like this the same way everyone one else did – by discounting to stimulate business. Unfortunately, what we found was that our loyal guests just got a better deal when we lowered the prices. Other guests taking advantage of the cheap rates didn't come back when prices went back to normal, as they couldn't afford the normal tariff.

We also found after each discounting period that it took us at least a year to get the prices back to where we needed them, so in October of 2008, when facing a disaster, we asked ourselves what else could we do to increase the value proposition of our product? Since we already included most things aboard, except spa, gift shop, casino, and tours, there was not much more we could do. Our research showed us that guests booked their cruise because of the destination. The guest satisfaction from the tours we sold was not as high as we would have liked, so we found a unique opportunity to add value and improve guest satisfaction. We basically decided to include all the tours we sold for $200 or less for free and charge a nominal cost for the more expensive tours or those that had a very limited capacity. We talked to the team who ran the tour programs and launched the scheme in January 2009. By the end of February 2009, we sold all 17 cruises where tours were included in the overall price. Based on those results, we launched the idea as an 'inclusive' feature and our recession ended in the first quarter of 2009. It was a real win: bookings got back to normal, guests were much happier with the ports they visited, and as the market improved our travel agent partners were able to use the 'inclusive' excursions as a tool to convert the much larger pool of experience cruises from the premium cruise lines. All of our competitors started copying our inclusive model, which showed how successful it was. It is hard to protect ideas once they are in the market, so what you have to do is constantly stay ahead of the rest.

We also changed the way we priced cruises. Most cruise lines launch the new season with higher prices and hold something back to use should the cruises not sell well. We did just the opposite by launching a new season with lower rates than we wanted to achieve, then raised our rates every quarter on cruises that were doing well. We therefore didn't require a lot of last minute discounting, since the consumers and their travel agents know the earlier they book, the better fares they receive."

How do you cope with stress?

"Stress does not really bother me as long as I can address what's causing it in the first place. Solving problems is very rewarding in its own right. You need to maintain a good sense of humor and try not to lose your temper unless that helps you get things done. Exercise tends to help keep me on an even keel, wherever possible. I was a competitive athlete in high school and college and find that what works best is to keep the goal in mind and focus on that instead of the problem. I just deal with it and try not to let it get to me. Some of my team would say I strive on stress. The other issue is to focus on your goals and look at stress as one of the obstacles that both helps and hurts you from reaching your goals. Losing is not an option, and coming from a big family has taught me how to cope.

The situation that causes me the most stress is letting people go. It is something I will never get used to. The other issue would be unreasonable people who you do everything for and they are still unhappy. I love to say yes and always try to find a win–win solution, but I have also fired my fair share of customers who just don't get it.

What qualities do I look for from employees? Aggressive decision makers who are also good team players. In my book, it is better to ask for forgiveness than permission as long as you use the proper thought process. Let's face it, most successful people are lucky to be right only about half the time. I had a mentor that told me it's good to be good but even better to be good and lucky. You still need a bit of luck to succeed, but in most cases you can help make your own luck by being prepared and working hard.

I have always been easily accessible to staff and have an open door policy. I sometimes forget to recognize people's success as much as I should. When I am angry I can be a bit intimidating and it's something I have to work on. Since I have had low-level jobs, I relate to our lowest ranking front line staff.

I like to inject humor into the workplace. If you don't have a sense of humor you should never get into the travel business. I love to tease and kid people I work with. My advice to people who find it difficult to cope with stress at work and at home is, to quote Winston Churchill: 'Do something you enjoy doing for a living and you will never work another day in your life.'

When I first started with RSSC, I worked constantly and missed much of my daughter's formative years. My wife and I always joke that Regent was our second child, but my daughter insists it was our first. My wife is also a successful executive in the industry and she understood why I had to work the way I do. I 'work hard, play hard', as do most of my close friends who are in the travel industry.

My advice to enterprising businessmen and women is to focus, work hard, and when you meet someone who is great at something, ask for their help. I would not be where I am today without the many mentors I had along the way.

The most important lesson I have learnt about business and life in general is to stay focused, work hard, be honest, and above all be kind. Remember that the people who work on your team and help you succeed are holding the ladder for you. Should you fail, they will be the ones who can help you restart."

ANALYSIS AND ADVICE

The issue of "being kind to others" keeps coming up in our interviews. If you create authentic and positive relationships with others, it can provide you with a "stress prevention inoculation," as many of the problems in the workplace are associated with people problems. Being yourself, treating people with respect, and being supportive and kind are critical characteristics of people who cope best with the pressures of work. As the Nobel Laureate Issac Bashevis Singer once wrote "Kindness, I've discovered, is everything in life." Second, as a manager, whether on the shop floor or top floor, it is important to delegate work to other people rather than keeping everything to yourself. Many senior people in the workplace try to do everything, but find after a period of time that they are unable to cope. Not only is delegating good for you by relieving "overload stress," but also it is "value/trust confirming" for the recipient, who can feel that you value and trust his or her expertise to manage that particular area, problem, etc.

Third, having professional training on communication skills is also a vital feature of people in business. Being able to listen to others and also to communicate emotional messages in the right way (e.g. telling someone they are being let go) is fundamental to minimizing stress in your and other people's lives. Lack of communications or inappropriate communications are frequently the cause of many stressful episodes in the workplace, so being forearmed is a useful stress prevention strategy.

chapter 13

Ann Widdecombe DSG – Former British Conservative Party Politician and Author

Ann Noreen Widdecombe (born 4 October 1947) is a former British Conservative Party politician and has been a novelist since 2000. She is a Privy Counsellor and was the Member of Parliament for Maidstone from 1987 to 1997 and for Maidstone and The Weald from 1997 to 2010. She was a social conservative and a member of the Conservative Christian Fellowship. She retired from politics at the 2010 general election. Since 2002 she has made numerous television and radio appearances, including as a television presenter. She is a convert from Anglicanism to Roman Catholicism. As an MP, Widdecombe was known for her strong, socially conservative views, including opposing the legality of abortion and supporting the reintroduction of the death penalty.

About Ann

"I was born in the first half of the last century in 1947, and at that time my family lived in Bath. As well as my mother and father, I had a grand-mother living with me until she died when I was 14 and an elder brother ten years older than me. My brother was born in Gibraltar before the War. I had a very happy childhood, but we moved around a lot. When I was about three we moved from Bath to Portsmouth because my father's job was to look after weapons for the Navy.

When I was five I went to the first of many schools, shortly before we moved to Singapore. In Singapore I was looked after by a Chinese nanny; then in 1956 I came back to England and for just a few months we lived at Tunbridge Wells in Kent, where I went to another school until we moved miles out in the country on Blackdown on the Surrey–Sussex borders. Two years later we moved again back to Bath, where I went to Bath Convent Prep School, then to Bath Convent Senior School – a very strict school – and we had to wear our uniform correctly at all times.

After I left Bath Convent, I went to Birmingham University to study Latin and after that I went to Oxford to study politics and economics. I always wanted to go into politics, and my first attempt at a seat was at Burnley in Lancashire. Burnley in those days still had a lot of miners and one of the things I had to do was go down a mine and crawl along on my knees and elbows because there was no room to stand up. I knew that it was going to be a matter of firstly establishing a record on the voluntary side, then fighting a seat. I fought Burnley, then fought a somewhat better seat at Devonport. This was very helpful as my father had a great many connections with Devonport, which had a very large naval dockyard. After Devonport, I stood in Maidstone, Kent and I represented the area for 23 years.

When the Conservatives were in power I was a Minister looking after first of all pensions, then employment, then prisons. When the Conservatives lost in 1997 I represented the Conservatives on matters concerning first of all health and then home affairs, which is the term we use to cover a variety of matters, including police, prisons, probation, immigration, fire, charities, etc. When the Conservatives also lost the last General Election I decided that I did not want to speak on just one thing anymore, and so I am now able to speak on many different things.

The enjoyment I got out of being an MP was the satisfaction of being able to influence things and being able to sort out problems for people. I enjoyed the cut and thrust of debate and in fact there wasn't much about the job that I didn't like. I suppose the most stressful aspect of the job was how the press have a habit of distorting anything to suit whatever agenda they are running at the time. There are very few people who go through life without encountering some degree of stress. I can't remember not being able to cope because of stress and it's never defeated me. If I was stuck in a rut, I would usually sleep on it or take a walk across the moors.

I think the important thing is to have a sense of humor. I would never have got through 'Strictly Come Dancing' otherwise. On the subject of 'Strictly', I am always being asked whether performing 'live' in front of millions of television viewers was stressful. It wasn't at all, as nothing depended on it. Everything I did when I was an MP, from the way I handled my work, to the way I voted in the House, to the policies I adopted as a Minister – whatever I did in Parliament had the potential to affect people in one way or another. Nothing I did on 'Strictly' could affect anything other than my dancing partner's (Anton du Beke) battered shins. It was utterly liberating to perform on the program and was ten weeks of sustained frivolity!

The key to being successful in life is to have confidence in whatever you do. This is more important than anything else. If you haven't got that and a sense of humor, then you're on a losing wicket.

Like most people in business, I have had setbacks. Mine started early in my career when I fought to get a seat. However, the right one always came up in the end, which usually happens.

I prioritized everything when I worked in Parliament, probably on an hourly basis. Things change so rapidly that you have to be ready to adjust to every situation. I don't prioritize these days as I've retired and there's no need to. I wish I was more disciplined in how many hours I spend working on my books. I work harder when there is a deadline to complete the book by.

I realize that some people find it hard to switch off from work. I never did. Now that I've retired, it's a lot easier as I work as and when I want to.

My advice to people thinking of going into politics is to think long and hard about it and don't do it until you have some experience of the world."

ANALYSIS AND ADVICE

There are lots of lessons to learn from someone who has been at the forefront of politics, particularly in a ministerial role. For many roles in life, the need for flexibility and the ability to prioritize one's workload is essential. There are different types of work overload: "quantitative overload," or just too much to do; and "qualitative overload," which is complex or difficult work to do. The former is easier to deal with, and being able to prioritize and micro-manage your workload is less difficult than having to deal with difficult people, or complex tasks, or the politics in the office, or having to tell people difficult things (e.g. they are going to lose their job).

A second issue that is intrinsic in some roles, like those of politicians, is the inevitable role conflict, because there are multiple and sometimes conflicting demands from constituents, the Party, the media, and one's own conscience – not much different for people working in a large organization! We are hearing now about the conflicts experienced by many healthcare professionals between their desire to spend time in their "caring role" with their patients and the demands of senior management in trying to keep the costs down, with the inevitable consequence of fewer staff and less time for healthcare professionals to do their pastoral care.

A third issue that emerges is the issue of determination. It is obvious that stress can occur when an individual is shifted in one direction or another, either by senior people or by circumstance, which undermines their capacity to focus on what they want to do. Being a determined person will help to focus on what needs to be done, but not all people have the "resilience" and determination to overcome all the obstacles in the workplace. Some people are just more resilient than others.

There are four characteristics of resilience: confidence, purposefulness, adaptability, and social support. Confidence is about having feelings of competence and effectiveness in coping with stress situations. Purposefulness is having a clear purpose, clear values, drive, and direction. Adaptability is about being flexible and adapting to changing situations which are beyond our control. And social support is building good relationships with others and seeking support when needed to overcome adverse situations (see Cooper *et al.*'s *Building Resilience for Success* book). (If you want to assess your own resilience check out the iResilience measure at *www.robertsoncooper.com*, which is free to users and gives you your own resilience profile).

chapter 14

Robert Barocci – President and CEO, Advertising Research Foundation (ARF), New York

In September, 2004, Robert Barocci was named President/CEO of the ARF. Just prior to joining the ARF, Bob was Director of Communications of New School University and part of Bob Kerrey's leadership team. Before that, he was "privileged to enjoy a very satisfying advertising career," including 21 years with Leo Burnett, culminating in the position of President of Leo Burnett International. After he left Leo Burnett, he was Founder/CEO of McConnaughy Barocci Brown, then invited by Alex Kroll to become Director of Central/East Europe for Young and Rubicam. He holds an MBA from Harvard University and a Phi Beta Kappa mathematics degree from the University of Wisconsin.

About Robert

"My early experiences in life were particularly good. We were a middle class family and I had wonderful parents and a great brother and sister. We lived in a small town, where I attended a local high school. I rarely got into trouble. I did well at school, got treated well, and have positive memories of my childhood.

My parents grew up poor in Northern Michigan in the copper mining country and my Dad was the first person in his town to go to college. My mother was pulled out of school at the age of 16 and had to go to work, as her family could not afford to feed four children. She never finished high school and was sent off to be a nanny far from home. My father was a very successful high school teacher – 42 years at the same school. I went to graduate school and eventually got into business and ended up earning very good money through the course of my life. My mother instilled in me that if I didn't succeed, I wasn't worth much. I had to perform in order to be valued.

I did well academically, being my high school salutatorian, and became a Phi Beta Kappa at the University of Wisconsin. I also got an MBA from Harvard. I was a Mathematics major in undergraduate school. This, together with my Harvard MBA, helped me to be very successful in my career. I joined the Leo Burnett Company, Inc. as soon as I graduated from Harvard and stayed there for 21 years.

I decided what career I wanted to pursue when I was at Harvard Business School. I wanted to have a job in marketing and the Leo Burnett advertising agency was hiring for the summer so I joined them, loved the company, and they gave me a job.

I have hardly been under much stress during the 40 plus years I have worked in business. I don't believe stress is necessarily part of the job. Successful executives experience very little stress. If your work is continuously stressful, then my advice is to get out, as stress affects performance and judgement and you cannot function properly. Maybe my behavior is such that I have managed to keep myself relatively stress-free. One thing that helped was maintaining my fitness and becoming a very competitive Masters runner. The most stressful time in my career occurred when I had a small business and the bank was closing in on the loans. Luckily I managed to sell the company and got through the crisis.

To me, the more stressful a situation, the more I like it. Give me a problem and I'll solve it. I learnt a whole lot of principles over the years which taught me how to cope with tough situations which I practise and continue to do regularly.

In 1976, after 11 years working at Leo Burnett, Chicago, I was sent to run Leo Burnett's London office, which was the biggest office outside of

Chicago but in the midst of a serious decline. I was 34 at the time and it was one of the biggest challenges of my career, as I had never run a company before and had to figure it out. It took me about six months to sort it out, which was a little stressful; however, it was undoubtedly the best time of my career. It was also my biggest business success to date, as the London agency had dropped out of the top ten to 13th in agency rankings. After three years, we managed to get it back to the seventh most popular agency. It was the first time that any agency had managed to achieve getting back to the top ten after dropping out.

I tend to micro-manage the things that need to be micro-managed. It's basically setting priorities and at the same time having a crystal-clear strategy in mind which guides everything you do – both of which are key.

I would say the thing that totally guides me is the ability to believe in myself. Secondly, as a boss you have to understand there's only a certain amount of accolades to go round and that they should go to the people who support the team and deserve them. Being a boss is an accolade itself. It's hard for egomaniacs to learn that you don't take the credit when you are the boss and that you have to leave it for more deserving people. The biggest enemy in business is egos, which lead to lots of bad management decisions.

In the service business, which I have spent my entire life in, the two most important factors in business success are (1) integrity and (2) to get your clients to trust you.

You must have the courage to take risks with no fear of failure. I learn more from failures than I do from successes. Failure means you have failed to do your job properly; however, the important thing is not to be disappointed but to find out where you went wrong. I remember reading about the CEO of Avis, who had written a book about his time with the company. He said that two out of every three decisions he made were wrong, but that he learnt from each mistake, which helped him to make the company successful.

When it comes to investments, if we decide to do something then we spend whatever money that's required to get it done. If you succeed, you succeed and if you fail, you fail. I don't prioritize daily; however, I do prioritize regularly. Every quarter I write down what the priorities should be and deal with them the best way I can.

Keeping the business fresh is critical in being a good boss and I think about that all the time. I am not a believer in brainstorming sessions as I think they are generally a waste of time. What I do is get the brightest people together in a room and collectively figure out the best way to deal with problems. Defining the problem is always the first objective of these meetings. 'A problem defined is a problem half-solved.' I always try out ideas on different target markets to see if they work and never think about protecting current business interests. It has probably cost me over the years. However, I don't pre-occupy my mind with that stuff. I'm constantly raising the bar for hitting higher targets and growing the company on a daily basis. That's a huge part of a CEO's job, which is why we rarely win popularity contests.

I agree that timing is important, as is the ability to predict the future. The market is constantly changing and things that worked last year won't necessarily work this year. Timing is critical in the sense that if you are in a competitive product category you have to lead – so by the time your competitors have matched what you are doing you have already moved on to something else. That's the kind of timing I'm referring to.

In my younger days, I found it impossible to switch off, but I am over that period. I now probably work eight hours a day and try not to work during the weekends. In the old days, I would usually work 15 hours a day, including weekends.

I have thankfully never lost the ability to cope in business, as I am usually prepared for everything. The things that cause me stress are unexpected situations or things that are outside my immediate control – for example, when the bank threatened to close my account unless I paid the loan off and not having money to pay off the debt for my small business. That's stressful!

When it comes to my staff, I look for extremely high standards of performance from each employee. My responsibility is to make sure they know what is expected of them and to make them aware of the consequences if they don't come up to expectations. I always give them a few chances, and if they still don't deliver, then they have to go.

I try to be very approachable; however, many staff over the years describe me as 'intimidating'. However, I don't see myself as that. Any staff member that comes to see me tends to have a pretty satisfactory conversation, but not every staff member is willing to do that.

I definitely try to inject humor into the workplace as and when required. It is a great stress release for people who need it and makes me feel human.

When people ask me how they can be successful in business, I outline the things that have worked for me. Fundamentally speaking you have to have the right personal values, integrity, compassion, and conscience. If you don't have them, you can't expect to succeed.

One regret I have from my impatient, younger days is firing the guy that I put in place to replace myself to run the London Leo Burnett office. I lost my patience with him too early and he went on to be quite successful elsewhere. Some years ago, the decision I used to regret the most is that I decided to leave Leo Burnett after 21 years. It was yet another bit of impatience, as I thought I could run the company at 44 years old. Others felt differently. As time went on, I quickly learnt that this decision opened up a lot of the world to me that I would not have had otherwise seen. It turned out to be the right thing to do, as my life is much fuller. Poorer, but filled with experiences like working in Central and Eastern Europe and numerous entrepreneurial ventures, plus ten years in a very satisfying job as President/CEO of the ARF."

ANALYSIS AND ADVICE

There are a number of generic qualities of working life lessons in this interview. The first is that the "biggest enemy in business is egos," when senior people believe their own press. Cultures based on "egos" are usually command and control ones, where people have little autonomy and engagement is minimal. Also in these environments there is usually little upward communication and people feel they can't provide constructive, negative feedback. This kind of culture is a breeding ground for workplace stress. In a recent Quality of Working Life survey for the Chartered Management Institute in the UK (professional body of managers), it was found that during the recession, the prevailing management style was autocratic and bureaucratic, having moved away from an engaging style (see Worrall and Cooper, *Quality of Working Life*, 2012).

The second lesson is that "integrity and trust" are keys to effective working relationships, and a more open and collegiate climate at work. As long as there is a bedrock of trust, people will be enabled to take the risks that business requires without fear of failure. Fear of failure usually leads to lack of innovation and people behaving in such a risk-averse way that it has significant negative consequences for the performance of the business, and also encourages in the staff less openness and sharing of information and experience. As James Bryant Conant once wrote: "behold the turtle: he only makes progress when he sticks his neck out."

The third lesson is about getting good work/life balance. Investing in your outside relationships minimizes the dangers associated with work spilling over into your home life and infecting your relationships there, as well as not providing you with the psychological and emotional respite needed to recover from the constant everyday stresses and strains of the workplace. We all need rest and recuperation. As John Ruskin, the social reformer, wrote in 1851, "in order that people may be happy in their work, these three things are needed: they must be fit for it, they must not do too much of it, and they must have a sense of success in it."

chapter 15

Ken Hom OBE – International Celebrity Chef, TV Presenter, and Author

Born 3 May 1949, Ken Hom resides in France and Thailand and travels tirelessly all over the world. He continues to appear regularly on TV as a celebrity chef, write new books, and keep an involvement with restaurants worldwide.

In 2007, he was awarded an honorary doctorate from Oxford Brookes University for his "outstanding success within the international food world" and to recognize him as one of the world's most notable chefs with a highly successful career in the media, as an entrepreneur, and as a supporter of charity and education. He was then appointed as Founding Patron of Oxford Gastronomica, the Centre for Food, Drink and Culture at Oxford Brookes University. Since 2008, Ken has become an ambassador for Action Against Hunger (www.aahuk.org), the humanitarian charity which works in over 40 countries helping families to feed their children and build a sustainable life.

Widely regarded as one of the world's greatest authorities on oriental cooking, Ken was awarded an honorary OBE in 2009 for "services to culinary arts," recognizing his achievements and the impressive social and historical impact he has made on the way the UK has "adopted" Chinese cuisine, which has become one of the nation's favorites. In November 2009, he launched his own range of Chinese meals exclusively for Tesco. Of high quality and with no additives, the range now comprises 30 dishes.

Ken has written 36 books, many translated into more than 15 languages, and has presented four television series – "Hot Chefs," "Ken Hom's Hot Wok," "Ken Hom's Foolproof Chinese Cookery" and "Travels with a Hot Wok," which attracted millions of viewers. His books include Exploring China: A Culinary Adventure and 100 Easy Chinese Suppers, which was published for www.mykitchentable.co.uk.

Born in Tucson, Arizona, where his Cantonese father lived after emigrating to America in the 1930s, Ken moved to Chicago with his mother after his father's death. As he grew up, he found American food unpalatable compared to his mother's cooking and she used to send him to school with a flask of hot rice and stir-fried vegetables.

Aged 11, he went to work in his uncle's restaurant, where he earned the equivalent of 30 pence per day. At 20, he headed off to California to study art history and French history. To pay for his university fees, he started to give cookery lessons and quickly realized that this was where his heart lay – especially with his native Chinese cuisine. He soon started teaching, first in his home, and then at the California Culinary Academy (a school for professional chefs in San Francisco). He also travelled to France and Italy to explore gastronomy further.

About Ken

"I was born of Chinese immigrant parents. My father died when I was eight months old, and shortly after my mother moved to Chicago, where relatives were able to find work for her. She never spoke English during her lifetime.

Originally my parents both came from prosperous families in southern China. The war with the Japanese wreaked havoc with their land holdings and all land was confiscated by the communists during the land reform. By the time my mother went to the US the family was impoverished.

I grew up very poor. However, the motivation to be successful was to make my mother proud.

Going to university opened a whole new world to me. I have always more or less worked for myself.

At the age of 11, I went to work for my uncle, Paul, who had one of the most successful restaurants in Chicago's Chinatown. He became my surrogate father and taught me how to cook, work, and save.

I worked in a number of jobs, including a brief spell in a supermarket and also as a messenger in an investment company office. I really had no clue about which career I wanted to pursue. My career just sort of fell into place.

The six key points in being successful in business are:

1. Listen.
2. Know when you are wrong.
3. Be open to new ideas.
4. Being humble goes a long way.
5. Share your success.
6. Smile.

I've learnt from successes and failures and my biggest setback in business has been over-reaching by over-expanding. I've always managed to get my business back on track by downsizing. My best business investment is the latest technology and my worst investment is wasting money on equipment that I've never used. I base all my business decisions on gut instinct and my biggest success to date is my BBC TV series, together with the books that have accompanied the series.

I am a very prudent spender and conservative investor and learn to expect the unexpected all the time. If I'm stuck in a rut and can't resolve a problem, I go away from the problem, refresh myself, and come back later to face it again. What strategy do I use? Chill-out! I don't believe you can always protect your ideas: the more the merrier. As for achieving bigger targets, I'm not really interested on getting bigger at this point in my life.

Timing is important in business, as is being in the right place at the right time. When my first BBC series came out in 1984, it was a huge hit because of the timing. I think my *East meets West* book came out too prematurely, before the market was ready for the idea, otherwise it would have been a bigger hit.

One of the worst moments of my life was discovering I had cancer. My initial reaction was one of shock. No one wants to find out they have a time bomb in their body, and when the doctor says you've got it, you just freeze. It was completely unexpected. I swim almost daily, eat a healthy diet, drink lots of green tea, and had no symptoms, so cancer was the last thing on my mind.

I was diagnosed in March 2010 following a routine annual check-up in Thailand, where I spend a lot of my time.

My cancer was an aggressive form of the disease, although it was luckily contained within the prostate gland. Like all men diagnosed with prostate cancer, I faced a difficult decision over which treatment option would be best for me. I opted to have Proton, a radiotherapy treatment, and had to undergo 37 sessions in two months. I was lucky as they caught the cancer early. Another year on and it may well have been too late. Every man thinks cancer can't happen to them, but it can, and we all need to have regular health checks.

Luckily, I emerged from the treatment without any side-effects, although I have regular PSA [prostate-specific antigen] tests to keep an eye on the situation. It is terribly important to catch aggressive prostate cancer early. All men need to know that prostate cancer exists. Let's not walk around with blindfolds on and let machismo be the death of us."

How do you cope with stress?

"I believe in a good work/life balance and think it's important to take time out to relax and enjoy life. My solution for coping with stress is to laugh. It releases stress so that you can think clearly. What causes me stress are deadlines. My advice to people who find it difficult to cope with stress at work and at home is to get away from work if that's what causing the stress. I find a good evening of food and wine with friends a fantastic way to cope.

The qualities that I look for from my employees are that they are motivated and passionate. I am always accessible to staff. I engage people to work with me on specific projects and if I ever had to fire anyone, I would always want to wish them success no matter where they go or what they do in the future. I think humor is essential in the workplace. I personally cannot stand a too serious environment or lots of whinging.

My advice to aspiring chefs, restaurateurs, and entrepreneurs is to be as open as you can to learning your profession. Observe and listen and you'd be surprised what you can learn. We are in a people business, so your relationship to others is important. The most important lesson that I've learnt about business is how difficult it can be, but equally rewarding. I would do things the same way if I started from scratch.

Ken Hom tips:

Be humble – The more you learn, the more you realize how little you really know. I am always surprised by new tastes and flavors, and I feel that life is a continuous learning process. The only time you stop learning is when you die. When death comes, as sure as the Sun comes up, we'll know how insignificant we really are in this universe. A humbling thought indeed.

True communication comes from gentle persuasion. That is one reason why I never shout in the kitchen. I don't like being shouted at and I never do it to others. I try to explain and convince those who work with me why my method deserves serious consideration. However, I am always open to other opinions as well. Then I add doses of lightness and humor. After all, is life that serious? It is amazing how laughter can conquer. It makes you feel better, as well.

Openness is a virtue. No matter what age you are, you should be open to new ideas. You don't have to like them all, but give yourself the opportunity to be convinced by those you do like. For example, there are some new trends in food I am not exactly crazy about, but my mind and palate are not closed to these trends."

ANALYSIS AND ADVICE

Some really good tips about managing stress come out of this interview. First, a great deal of conflict at work and in life more generally comes from people just not listening to others. Theo Theobald and Cary Cooper, in their book *Shut Up and Listen*, suggest ways in which listening might help in communications at work: listening not only to the words, but to the emotions that underpin them; making eye contact; signal to the person that you are hearing what they are saying by nodding and smiling; repeat back what you think they have said if you are unclear about what they are saying; avoid the temptation to jump in with solutions, when you haven't fully explored the problem; and "for every minute that you talk, spend two listening." The aviator Charles Lindbergh once said "Isn't it strange that we talk least about the things we think most about."

Second, temporarily step away from a problem or relationship difficulty that you are having trouble with, and come back to it afresh at a later date. Relationship problems particularly create stress and prevent you from doing your job properly, as well as causing ill health effects. This was known as far back as AD 140, when the Roman emperor Marcus Aurelius wrote:

> Don't waste the rest of your time here worrying about other people – unless it affects the common good. It will keep you from doing anything useful. You'll be too preoccupied with what so-and-so is doing, and why, and what they're saying, and what they're thinking, and what they're up to, and all the other things that throw you off and keep you from focusing on your own mind.

The third lesson is about the work/life interface, the imbalance of which causes many people enormous problems in their life as they juggle work and family demands. Given the long working hours cultures in many organizations and many jobs, the spill-over effect on families and work intruding into one's personal life has become a major issue. Ensuring that there is sufficient space for your personal and family needs is fundamental. Although "work at least gives him a secure place in a portion of reality in the human community," as Freud wrote in his book *Civilization and Its Discontents*, many of the interviewees in this book seem haunted by the effect that work and success have on their private life and family, as I found in an earlier book I co-wrote, entitled *The Change Makers*. I get the same feeling here, where we are hearing about the importance of their family as their "social support team," which can be undermined, in today's world, by technology accessing people whenever and wherever they are, interfering with that precious time with their loved ones and close friends.

And finally, there is the issue of humility, of knowing your own weaknesses and ensuring that you stay rooted to who you are and to your past experiences, and never believing your own "success press."

chapter 16

Sir Chris Bonington CVO, CBE, DL – World-Famous Mountaineer, Explorer, and Writer

Chris Bonington, mountaineer, writer, photographer, and lecturer, started climbing at the age of 16 in 1951 and it has been his passion ever since. He made the first British ascent of the North Wall of the Eiger and led the expedition that made the first ascent of the south face of Annapurna, the biggest and most difficult climb in the Himalaya at the time. He went on to lead the successful expedition making the first ascent of the south west face of Everest in 1975 and then reached the summit of Everest himself in 1985 with a Norwegian expedition. He is still active in the mountains, climbing with the same enthusiasm as he had at the beginning.

He has written 17 books, fronted numerous television programs, and has lectured to the public and corporate audiences all over the world. He received a knighthood in 1996 for services to mountaineering, was president of the Council for National Parks for eight years, is Non-Executive Chairman of Berghaus, and Chancellor of Lancaster University.

About Chris

"My parents split up when I was very young. My father left my mother to bring me up on her own without any financial support. They had met at Oxford and my Mum worked as a copy writer. I was sent to boarding school at the age of five to get me out of London at the start of the war. I returned to London at the age of eight to go to a day school in Hampstead, then to University College School. I loved history but was not much good at games. However, I ended up as captain of the *Third* XV at rugby – all the guys who were very enthusiastic but not much good. This was my first leadership role.

My parents were middle class. My mother was able to make just enough money in advertising to put me through University College School, Hampstead. However as soon as I was off her hands, she changed to teaching English in a secondary school, which was something she loved doing. My mother encouraged my love of reading. I'd read many of the classics by the age of 13, when I became fascinated by military history and most of my reading in my teens was directed in that direction. Mum had to send me off with friends or to farm schools during the holidays and I think this encouraged independence.

I was quite academic at school and won a prize for history in the Junior Sixth. I had already discovered rock climbing at the age of 16, which was my passion, but never thought that I could make a living around it. I had a place at University College London, but fluffed one paper in English A levels and couldn't face another year at school, so went off to do my National Service in the Royal Air Force (RAF), hoping to get into Mountain Rescue. Because I'd been to a public school it was suggested I should apply for a commission. I went the whole hog and applied for a regular commission which took me to the RAF College Cranwell training to be a pilot. I was no good at flying, but I liked the life and wanted to be in a fighting arm, and so transferred to Sandhurst to be commissioned into the Royal Tank Regiment. This at least showed flexibility and a determination to do something I really wanted to do.

I had my first real experience of leadership as a troop commander in charge of 12 men and three tanks. I made a lot of mistakes and learnt a huge amount – that leadership doesn't depend on the pips on your shoulder, but rather, the loyalty and respect you earn from the qualities you show your subordinates. At the end of two years I was a good troop commander. I then transferred to the newly formed Army Outward Bound School as an instructor, for my love of climbing. By this time, I was a very good rock climber and Alpinist and had my first Himalayan expedition, making the first ascent of Annapurna II, a peak of just under 8000 meters.

The following year, in 1961, I was invited to join a civilian expedition to Nuptse, the third peak of Everest. The army wouldn't let me, so I resigned my commission but took the precaution of getting the promise of a job as management trainee with Unilever on my return from the expedition and a long climbing summer in the Alps, making several attempts on the North Wall of the Eiger, and making the first ascent of the Central Pillar of Freney, high on the south side of Mont Blanc, at the time described as the last great problem of the Alps.

Unilever didn't last long. I had an invitation to join an expedition to Patagonia: I asked my sales director for leave of absence but he told me I needed to make a choice between a career with Unilever or a life around climbing. I chose the latter. I had just got married to Wendy; was not at all sure what I was going to do after the expedition, but thought I might try to get into university and become a teacher, to have long holidays for climbing.

I left Unilever at the start of the Alpine season of 1962, made some more attempts on the North Wall of the Eiger, and at the end of a long summer of uncertain weather, snatched the opportunity of a fine spell and climbed it before going off on the expedition to South Patagonia. So far I had not had a very successful career, but I had laid the foundations for what I was going to do in the future. I was commissioned to write my first book, *I Chose to Climb*, and began public lecturing. I put thoughts of going to university on hold.

Wendy and I were quite hard up in my early days as a freelancer. We were permanently overdrawn until I'd finished my book and had started doing a lot of work as an adventure photo-journalist. My work as a photo-journalist was interesting, challenging, and a very important learning process, both in my photography and ability to write. I was getting an increasing number of assignments from newspapers and magazines.

In 1969, when I started planning the Annapurna South Face Expedition, I realized that I preferred to be organizing and taking part in my own adventures rather than reporting those of others. This was the first time I had led an expedition and I enjoyed the challenge of planning, organizing, and leadership, though I made plenty of mistakes on the way, but learnt from them.

How did I cope with the physical and mental challenges of the incredibly difficult expeditions I've been on? It just came naturally – I was doing what I loved doing. I have come close to losing my life on many occasions; however, it never occurred to me at any point to give up climbing. I am good in crisis situations: keep cool and focus on getting out alive. Narrow escapes or epics have never put me off – if anything I find them stimulating. They are certainly useful to liven up a book or lecture.

My top tips for being successful are:

- Be passionate in what you do.
- Be prepared to work hard.
- Be clear, single minded and focused about your objective.
- Good planning and organization.
- Delegate effectively.
- Inspire your team and gain their loyalty and respect.
- Integrity

I've learnt from successes and failures. You have to take the rough with the smooth and not get over enamored with plaudits of success, or dispirited by setbacks.

I don't prioritize on a daily basis and I'm a bit disorganized on this score. If I'm stuck in a rut, I go for a walk in the hills behind our home. Teamwork is absolutely essential in any group effort, whether it's on a climb or in business.

I've lost all too many friends climbing, some of them on expeditions I have led. I have never become hardened to it; I grieve their loss and dread it happening again, yet if you want to go on climbing you've just got to accept it as part of the game you play.

I never push anyone on my climbing team to beyond what they are prepared to do. The important thing to remember is that essentially the mountain or the route that you are trying to climb has no huge importance to the future of mankind, so it's not worth putting pressure on anyone for that reason. I definitely believe in injecting humor on a tough expedition to relieve stress.

My advice to anyone keen to take up climbing is to do what you enjoy doing for the love of it rather than for the sake of getting famous.

I've enjoyed every moment of my career as a mountaineer and explorer. It has so many interesting facets, including the joy of climbing, the stimulus of risk, the fascination of exploration, the beauty of the mountains, and the friendships made."

ANALYSIS AND ADVICE

You can sense in this interview and for many of our other interviewees the significance of "passion" for what they do. There are people in jobs who see it only as a "living," rather than a vocation, and as a consequence are more likely to experience the stresses and strain of the modern workplace, and everything it can throw at them. Successful people and good "copers" seem to possess commitment and passion, which seems partly to be a natural "coping vaccine," enabling them to deal with the daily hassles of the job, and to put into context the more serious pressures they face to fulfill their ambitions.

Second, the importance of team building and leadership comes up again. Proper team building seems to provide the social supports that many people in high-pressure jobs need to achieve their objectives, particularly in the context of climbing or doing a major surgical operation or in bomb disposal work, where human life is at risk.

Third, it seems success and coping go hand in hand with people who grasp the opportunities, who take control, and don't allow events or circumstance to control them. George Bernard Shaw captured this in "Mrs. Warren's Profession": "People are always blaming their circumstances for what they are. I don't believe in circumstances. The people who get on in this world are the people who get up and look for the circumstances they want, and if they can't find them, make them.""

chapter 17

Angela Knight CBE – Chief Executive, Energy UK

Angela Knight is the Chief Executive of Energy UK and is also a non-executive director on the boards of Brewin Dolphin plc, Tullett Prebon plc, and Transport for London, and a member of the PwC Advisory Board.

Prior to joining Energy UK, Angela was Chief Executive at the BBA (British Bankers' Association) for five years. Before that she was Chief Executive of the Association of Private Client Investment Managers and Stockbrokers for nine years and was honored with a CBE for services to the financial services industry in 2007.

Angela was Economic Secretary to the Treasury from 1995 to 1997, after being Parliamentary Private Secretary to the Rt. Hon. Kenneth Clarke MP, Chancellor of the Exchequer, and before that to Industry Minister the Rt. Hon. Sir Tim Sainsbury MP. She was MP for Erewash from 1992 to 1997.

She graduated from Bristol University with a degree in chemistry and worked at Air Products before jointly setting up and running the company Cook & Knight Ltd for six years.

About Angela

"I went to seven schools, as my father moved around the country after my mother died when I was still a baby. This early life meant that I was used to having to deal with change, including being able to make friends easily, deal with different and sometimes difficult situations, and be relatively independent.

My father was a notable entrepreneur who built up a heavy industrial company in the North of England.

My school education was patchy. I mostly went to all-girls' schools at a time when expectations of girls were rather different than they are today. The key success was getting into Bristol University to read chemistry at a time when few girls actually got to Bristol and even fewer did science degrees. That was significant in providing a springboard for a 'non-traditional' female job when I left university in the early 1970s.

I joined Air Products, the international industrial gas company, as only their second ever female graduate trainee. After five years, I left to start a small specialist industrial company undertaking the heat treatment of ferrous metal components in Rotherham in South Yorkshire. Politics commenced as a part-time occupation as a Sheffield City Councillor and then became full-time after I was elected to parliament and the company I founded was sold. After losing my seat in 1997, I have since headed up three trade associations – APCIMS, BBA, and now Energy UK – and also undertaken a variety of non-executive director roles in a wide range of PLCs of all sizes.

I have therefore had more than one career! Engineering for approximately 15 years; politics for 10 years (including national and local government); financial services industry for 15 years; and now the energy industry from September 2012. None of this has been particularly easy and all have required persistence, hard work, and determination. Often this is because of the difficulty of the industry and the issues involved. The days are long, as is the commute (up at 5:30 a.m. and home by 7:30 p.m. on an early day). Then there's always the family things to be done, plus some house-work, and the food to be prepared.

One of the biggest challenges though was when I was given a project by Air Products Ltd that required working night shifts at Vauxhall Motors in Luton. I was 22 and very new to the role. The second major challenge was running the British Bankers' Association through the time of the biggest banking crisis of the last 100 years.

In terms of finding time to oversee and manage the various aspects of the work I do, it's a matter of having a retentive memory, keeping going, and doing without sleep, if necessary. If you get stressed with the work you do, often it either can be because it is the wrong job or it's outside your competencies.

If I can't resolve a problem, I try to have a good night's sleep, some exercise, then call a roundtable and thrash it out. I usually try out my ideas on different target markets to see if they work and mould and shape the project according to the response.

I've learnt from successes and failures. My biggest failure was losing my parliamentary seat in 1997, then having to change career. I am a risk taker, but do not rely on gut instinct. I am careful with budgets and seldom overspend. I do not go to bed until I have completed what needs to be done, and if an unexpected crisis arrives, it just means that I am awake longer.

The key points in being successful in business are to have a very clear strategy and execute it properly, never be afraid to say you are wrong and apologize, and look after your staff.

I am not necessarily always raising the bar or hitting bigger targets. In the occupations that I have been in, the bar is lifted all the time by others. Timing and luck are essential in business. Examples of bad timing for me were starting at the BBA just before the banking crisis (the crisis was not expected); and setting up the contract heat treatment business in Rotherham 18 months before the big recession of the end of the 70s and start of the 80s!"

How do you cope with stress?

"My advice to people who find it difficult to cope with stress at work and at home is to set sensible parameters, minimize aggressive timetables, ensure you get plenty of fresh air and exercise every day, think about how best to manage your job, and talk to someone about the problem.

The qualities I look for from people who work for me are enthusiasm, application, and intelligence.

I only get involved in hiring and firing when it becomes really difficult and I always seek an effective solution for the individual. I like to inject humor into the workplace. It's a necessary and normal part of work life.

My advice to enterprising businessmen and women is: do your homework thoroughly, keep a clear sense of direction and don't be discouraged by setbacks, and be objective. Always be fair in your dealings with others and make time for family and friends."

ANALYSIS AND ADVICE

The most important aspect that comes out of this interview is the notion of "high resistance to stress," which in psychological jargon is about "resilience." Resilience is basically how you adapt to adversity or stress, in effect possessing the coping strategies appropriate to the source of that stress. Resilience, as we discussed earlier, is comprised of several different characteristics: purposefulness, confidence, social support, and adaptability. Purposefulness is all about having a clear sense of direction, which we can see in this interview, a view of where an individual wants to go, and having the drive to get there.

Adaptability is about being flexible in achieving one's goals, a kind of bounce-back quality when things aren't going well or become overwhelming. Confidence is about feeling you have the capability of overcoming an obstacle: that you can deal with most obstacles that come your way. It is also about positivity, about seeing roadblocks or problems as an opportunity to do things differently rather than a "no-go" area. And finally social support, which is about building a social network that you can turn to when times get tough. This is very difficult for many successful people, because they are so committed to their careers and getting ahead that they don't tend to have enough time or emotional energy to invest in others. This aspect of resilience tends to be a weak point for many high-pressure people, whatever their walk of life.

A second characteristic that comes out of this interview is the need to deal with people who are enthusiastic, the "glass half full" types. One of the inoculating effects of stress is to choose to work with people who are positive and optimistic rather than "nay-sayers." The Roman Emperor Marcus Aurelius once wrote: "When you need encouragement, think of the qualities the people around you have: this one's energy, that one's modesty, another's generosity, and so on. Nothing is as encouraging as when virtues are visibly embodied in the people around us, when we're practically showered with them.""

chapter 18

Shelley Zalis – CEO, Ipsos Open Thinking Exchange

With over 25 years of experience working in traditional marketing and advertising research companies, Shelley Zalis held senior positions at ASI Market Research (now Ipsos ASI) and Nielsen Entertainment prior to founding OTX (Online Testing Exchange) in 2000. Under Shelley's vision and guidance as CEO, OTX became one of the largest (top 20) research companies in the world, amassing $60 million in revenue in just nine short years. It also became one of the savviest, known as a firm that would take risks and deliver robust, cutting-edge, technology-enabled solutions that few thought possible. In addition, Shelley became the first woman chief executive ranked in the top 25 of the largest research companies and devoted herself to becoming a mentor and friend to other women and leaders in the industry, set on shaking up what is often viewed as a very safe, very traditional world. In 2008, Shelley was awarded the Ernst & Young Entrepreneur Of The Year® award in the On-Line Services category and, in 2010, the ARF Great Minds in Innovation award.

In January 2010, OTX was acquired by Ipsos. Shelley now leads the Ipsos Global Innovation Center, Ipsos Open Thinking Exchange, pioneering next generation research solutions. Shelley is a highly sought-after keynote speaker at industry conferences around the world, sharing her vision on the Future of Research and "The New Normal."

Shelley continues to go against the grain to innovate and stimulate the industry. A pioneer, a wife, and a mother of three, she finds inspiration in her children to create new products and successfully juggles between CEO and Mom.

About Shelley

"I grew up in an incredibly supportive family, where my father was a cardiologist and my mother was working full-time, but for free. They were always busy, as president of the School Board and active members of foundations and charitable organizations. I grew up with three sisters and my parents always found a way to make each of us feel that we were amazing. They instilled confidence, love, and support in everything we did. If we came home with a B+ on our report card, they would say 'why didn't you get an A?' It was not to get an A for the sake of getting an A, but to be the best we could be. They wanted us to achieve anything we could imagine. And I think the most amazing thing for me is that even though I grew up in a home with a very comfortable lifestyle, it was a natural feeling for me to work and pay for myself, rather than take the easy way. In the summers when all my friends vacationed in Europe, I would hold two jobs, working at Universal Studios during the day and at the Greek Theater at night. Even though my parents never expected me to do that, it made me feel good and proud.

My parents were wealthy, but self-made. My father did not come from a wealthy family and was really a self-made person through education. Despite not having that role model in his life, he felt the need to be a professional and put himself through college and medical school. My mother came from a background where the husband works and the mother takes care of the family. She was an amazing role model to me – even though she didn't work a paid job, she was so inspiring with her organizations and foundations. When I went to college, she started working full-time because it was what she wanted … it was completely her choice.

I never thought I would be a career person. Instead, I pictured myself becoming a full-time mom and PTA president, just like my mother when

I was growing up. My jobs from college were always just jobs because, at the time, I never thought about my long-term career goals. I actually fell into my career when I was a senior at Columbia University. I aced my classes and had a lot of free time. So I felt the need to do something. I decided to get a job and found something that seemed like an ad agency. I got dressed up in a suit and took the subway to my interview. I still have a vivid memory of dropping my purse in the subway rail and having to bend down to get it … and then completely ripping my panty hose in the process. I showed up at the interview a complete mess! When I got to the office, I saw these three women chatting and laughing and I immediately thought 'Wow! This seems like a great place to work – I can do this!' I met with the boss – his name was Dave Vadehra – and he hired me on the spot. It turned out that this company was not an ad agency on any level. Rather, it was a mall intercept market research company, where we did communications testing using video story boards.

Well, I ended up falling in love with the business and I stayed at this company for eight years. I loved it there! It was a really relaxed environment. I typed on a typewriter and had hands-on experience with clients. There were a lot of things about this company and this job that, at the time, I didn't realize how much I appreciated. Dave used to have this jar called the 'brilliant idea jar'. There were only six people in the office and any time one of us had a brilliant idea, we put it in the jar. Every week, we sat around and would open up the jar and talk about the ideas. I really loved that and I had no idea that work could be any different or that the business world was not really like that.

I didn't realize at the time that having access to the CEO and President of the company was so unusual. I talked to Dave, the President, every day. He always asked for suggestions and ideas and I was a very important player in his world. I loved it and I loved the opportunity of working with the largest clients. When I eventually got recruited by a head hunter to interview for a quantitative research position for ASI, I remember walking into Dave's office, telling him about the ASI job, and asking him what quantitative research is. He started laughing and explained that quantitative is what I have been doing all these years, but on a big scale – it was talking to a lot of people. I told him that I needed to go and spread my wings to explore other opportunities. He agreed and, with his blessing, I went to the interview.

When I met with the chairman of ASI, he sat me down, showed me two television commercials for Domino's Pizza, and asked me which one I thought tested better. I was so excited for this challenge – this was in my blood and I was confident that I knew how consumers think. I picked the right commercial and he hired me immediately. I went from a salary of below $50,000 to one that was six figures in a year … and I couldn't believe someone would pay me that much money to do what I loved to do. The ASI chairman asked me what I needed for my job and I said two things – a television to watch ads on and a typewriter. He gave me the TV and, instead of a typewriter, he gave me a computer.

I found that when I got to ASI, it was a very competitive environment. Unlike my previous job, ASI felt like a big company where you had to find your own angle. I quickly discovered that what I loved doing was developing relationships with clients, listening to their real needs, and determining how research could benefit their business. My ultimate goal was to help each of my clients get home early and look good to their boss – which, in turn, would make them love me because I helped them become so important in their organization.

One of the most important things I learnt was to never wait for clients to call me for a project. Instead, they became my friends, whether there was a project or not. I was working with them because of our continuous conversation and collaborative brainstorming. I found my rhythm and entered the world of business development and client relationships.

I was not academic at all – in fact, I hated studying. I loved people more. What was so great about Columbia was that I was meeting many diverse people from different cultures and different parts of the world. I was fortunate to find classes where I didn't have to be in the library, because what I loved most about my education was my interactions and relationships with people. Strangely enough, I had no idea that I would end up in market research, where it's all about understanding people and uncovering what makes them tick. And, later in life, I realized how relevant my psychology major was.

My parents loved, encouraged, and supported me ... they were really there for me. Especially now, as I am a workaholic, they are always there to support me. My career is a choice – I work because I love what I do and it's a passion for me. I really do promote the work/life balance. While I think it's so important to do something you enjoy doing, I strongly believe that it should not be at the sacrifice of your family. You need to have your priorities straight – be connected, have a connected family, and have it all.

Deciding on what career to pursue wasn't really a decision – it was an 'Aha!' moment for me. When I worked at ASI, it was a really corporate organization and I used to get in trouble all the time. My bosses were critical of my expense reports because I always took clients out to lunch and dinner ... being in business development, I always believed in in-person interaction and bringing clients together. I really don't think my bosses understood the importance of the relationships I was developing with clients. Today, 28 years later, I have the same relationships with those clients because of the time I've spent with them over the years. I know when their birthdays are, what their interests are, where they've travelled, and what their children are into.

I came up with an idea to migrate research to the Internet in a day and age where no one was online except for wealthy old men over the age of 55 with broadband connections. Hardly a representative population for research! When I suggested this idea, the executive board of ASI (all men) told me it was too premature. Their first focus needed to go from being a US-based company to a global organization. I remember going home that night and thinking to myself, 'Why are they always right? And I'm not?' and 'Why can't I move in a direction that I believe is right?' The next day, I went in and resigned. I realized that my calling was to build my own research company. It was my moment of truth and I needed to pursue this dream. My heart was beating so fast! If I didn't move forward with this, no one else would. I just couldn't believe that I had an idea that no one else had and that I was the first to pioneer it. My entire life and career changed from that moment forward."

How do you cope with stress?

"One of the most important things that I always promised myself is to never look back at my life and have regrets. So, I look forward and I make decisions based on 'Will that bother me if I do it?' and 'Will I feel bad that I didn't do this and I didn't do that?'

Coping with pressure and stress is also about being realistic about what you can do and about not pushing yourself to do more than you can. I also integrate my girlfriends in the things in my life that I need to do anyway. I have breakfast with my girlfriends; we work out and get our nails done together. That way, it's never a choice between me and my girlfriends. I also invite my children and my husband to join me whenever they can when I travel. All my clients know that my work is a hobby and a lifestyle and my family will always come first. It's all about balancing choices.

I enjoy challenging projects and have built a lot of firsts. I'm actually a pioneer in building firsts. The challenges are in building a business model that doesn't exist. It's very challenging to build a budget around an unknown and then have to deliver something you made up. I think the greatest challenge was having a vision and creating a road map in a virgin territory and then getting people to follow and trust you. That has been the greatest challenge … and, it has also been the greatest reward. You really learn the importance of trust and relationships, along with the value of partnership, when you hold hands and jump off the cliff together. It's a lot more fun when you go together. So I think the greatest challenge is the unknown and the greatest reward is the unknown.

Finding time to oversee and manage everything is always a challenge. I think the biggest trick is realizing that you can't do everything and you need to empower people. For me, people are the greatest asset I have ever had. So, the more you groom, mentor, and lead your team towards leading themselves, the better off you'll be in terms of scale and growth. The other thing that I've always done is give – I didn't make the company about me. Any time press would call, I would transfer them to different people and build the reputation of the company on many different people. I built the image around the company so that it wasn't a 'Shelley Zalis' company, but rather a company filled with people who have passion and real innovation and inspiration.

To me, there are eight things that drive success in the workplace:

1. Work/life balance and knowing that work isn't life and everything is about choices.
2. Passion for what you do.
3. Relationships with your clients and not just when they're giving you business.
4. The people that you work with. Teamwork and collaboration – there is no 'I' or 'me' … it definitely is a 'we'. When people say 'I did this' or 'I did that', you know that they aren't a good team player.
5. Never take no for an answer – there's always a yes, you just have to find it.
6. Be a champion of your own destiny – be a champion of change if you're a change agent, because no one will make your bed … *you* have to make it.
7. Create a happy work culture.
8. Never have regrets. Always follow your gut and your heart. Never sacrifice the things that are important to you, because you can't get them back.

I have learnt from successes and failures and share all of my failures. I always say that when you fail, it means you're trying something new. So, failure leads to success. I just say don't make the same mistakes twice. And, I don't make dumb mistakes. Typos are dumb and unacceptable because they are careless. Make smart mistakes, big mistakes, small mistakes. Don't hide them, because they will always come back and haunt you and, when they do, you won't be able to fix them. Share and be open. When you mess up, have someone help you fix it. I share all my failures because I think you learn from them. It's very easy to talk about the things you do right. But, you learn the most from the things you do wrong *if* you're willing to admit that you have done stuff wrong. Just fix it and move forward.

My biggest setback in business was in the early days of building and pioneering online research, when security of content was a very big issue. I tested things before they hit the air and once had a very big movie trailer stolen. And, to make matters worse, it went viral. This was many, many years ago and, of course, a movie can close before it even opens. So, I got a call on a Friday night and it was a disaster. I actually thought I was never going to work in the movie business again. As it turns out, it was terrible, but it was a good bad. I told the client that the bad news is someone hacked it and the good news is that it took over a 100 people collectively more than 24 hours to break in. This forced me to build a new DRM solution to protect the content we test. Microsoft and all those people weren't going to build a DRM solution for a little research company, so it forced me to do that. This was an opportunity, as well as a really interesting precursor to how great it is sometimes when things go viral. It was a terrible thing at the time, but I had no one to follow and I had no idea that something like that could possibly happen. But, it ultimately turned into a really good experience.

I've always taken risks in business and don't think I've ever played it safe. I'm known as the black sheep everywhere I go. But I think black is the new white. I think if you don't take risks, there's no reward. Playing it safe today will get you nowhere. You know, we're in a day and age of constant transformation and, if you don't change, you'll become irrelevant. I continue to base my decisions on gut instinct.

The thing I'm the most proud of is my children. My biggest business success was pioneering online research in the industry and creating OTX.

When it comes to budgets, I always build what I need to, then think about the budget. If I thought about the budget first, I would be safe. I always start by thinking about what needs to get done. And then, when I decide that I need to do it, I do it in the most financially responsible way. But if I allowed numbers to drive my thinking, I would have never built most of the things that I have built. So I actually think first and then build the business model around it, versus the other way around.

On the subject of prioritizing work, I'm very non-linear. I'm OCD, so I can't leave something undone. I don't start things that I don't want to do because I don't like tedious work. I won't touch them because, once I touch them, I have to finish them. And, I won't start something that doesn't interest me because it's just a waste of time for me. I will move where the wind blows me if I feel that I have to go in that direction. And I surprise people all the time, including myself.

Implementing work changes: I believe in 'do' and then 'learn' versus 'learn' and then 'do'. If you think too much, you won't do anything. So, I think you have to push and then see – that really is my motto. But, if you change all the time, there's no consistency. I think you always have to be open-minded and push forward. And, once it's sticky, you have to go deep and develop it. However, I also believe that organizational structure needs to evolve. I have always built a fluid and flexible organizational structure to be able to adapt to changing times and the changing needs of our clients and the marketplace.

I never get stuck in a rut. I always talk about stuff and I share everything. I'm very transparent. I have no secrets. I think that sharing with someone, whether it's needing someone to listen or getting feedback, is the best way to go. I don't think that anything solves itself, unless it really is a passing phase. But, if it's something that really is an issue and a problem, it will require some kind of active engagement.

I work with clients on their business needs and take them to the next level. Everything I have ever done has been based on client need and client discussion. If you build it with your clients, then obviously they are going to buy it because they helped you build it. They need it and it makes them smarter. I don't know why more people don't do that!

In terms of raising the bar for hitting bigger targets, I raise the bar for myself. I don't raise it for anyone else. I am my own competition and the bar might not be a financial bar, it may be a personal bar. But there always has to be a challenge that you create for yourself or you will never evolve.

If *you* don't push yourself, no one will push you. So, I create my own pushes and I compete with myself.

Timing is crucial in business. If you're going to do it, do it now … what are you waiting for? Being first is never a good position, because you're the one who will make all the mistakes. And, being second is just following the leader … you'll do it a little bit better, but you're still going to make a lot of mistakes. Being third is always the best because you get to walk, ride, or run on the coat tails of #1 or #2 and take credit for all the good things. However, I can't imagine waiting to be third when I really am first. And, if I am the first to think about it, it would give me terrible stress and anxiety if I couldn't go to market with the idea. If someone else did it, it would kill me if I waited and it wasn't me.

I never allow stress to overwhelm me and I manage my way through each situation. Yes, I'm always racing for an airplane and that's stressful. Nowadays I've stopped running – I'm either going to make the plane or I'm not going to make the plane. Nothing is that important.

My advice to people suffering with stress is don't take life so seriously. Break things into sound bites and take life one step at a time. Most people think that everything is either black or white and they make their problems much bigger than they really are. They should break them into chunks and work their way through them step-by-step. They'll see that it's just not as bad when it's not just one giant step.

Motivation in life has to come from within. You know, a lot of people can tell you that you need to go on a diet. However, if you don't feel it, it doesn't matter how many people tell you something. So, while motivation comes from within, I think inspiration does come from another place. I think it starts with your 'leader', who inspires you to want to do great things. Then you want to do them for yourself and no one is going to babysit you. What I really look for in people is that they are passionate, curious, and willing to discover – people who say 'I can do this', 'I can', and 'I will'. They raise their hand and take the first step, always coming up with ideas, whether they are little ideas, big ideas, stupid ideas, good ideas. The fact that they have ideas and they share them is what matters. Collaboration, team, intuition, street smarts, understanding people, relationships, and caring. I want people who care about what they do. I don't just want employees, I want people who really care and treat what they're doing as their own.

When it comes to injecting humor into tense work situations, I think choco- late is the secret to success. People call me a character and I really think I'm like a caricature. I didn't realize I was until I walked in and saw employees playing one of those video games and I was actually a character in one of them. They had me in my big sunglasses, my high heels and my little Hermes bag, and wearing a straight little skirt that I could barely move in. So, I guess I am funny and I'm a caricature because I'm not like everyone else. But, I'm not a funny person and I don't really use humor in that way.

My advice to enterprising businessmen and women is that things don't happen just because you want it to happen. It happens when it happens. A lot of kids come out of school thinking that they're going to run a company and be an entrepreneur. And that when they have a good idea, it transforms into a big company. The truth is that it takes a lot of work, a lot of commitment, and a lot of iteration. Success needs to happen in every aspect. You could be successful financially, but if the other parts in your life don't work, you will not be successful. Success is happiness and not just monetary. You could have all the money in the world and not be happy, and then you won't be successful. I think you have to understand that it is hard work and you're going to put a lot of time into it, so you have to find ways to love it. There are always ways to create that game within yourself that, in turn, creates new thresholds to achieve.

The most important lessons I have learnt about business is love what you do. Be happy and balance your life. Never sacrifice anything that is important to you because it won't come back later."

ANALYSIS AND ADVICE

There are many gems for managing high pressure in this interview. The first is the advice to those suffering from stress "not to take life so seriously," which means contextualizing your problems in terms of the broader aspects of your life. You may lose a customer or have a budget reduced, but it is not like having a close relative with a life-threatening disease. Most of the everyday stresses and strains in our working lives are caused by an accumulation of minor events rather than something job- or life-threatening.

Second, many of our interviewees have talked about building teams and how significant that is in terms of a workplace social support system, but what is really important is making sure that the team gets the credit and not you! As Lao Tzu wrote regarding Taoist philosophy "a leader is best when people barely know he exists. When his work is done, his aim fulfilled, people will say 'we did it ourselves'."

Third is the issue of delegation and empowering people to do their job. Fundamental to all healthy workplaces is the issue of people feeling valued and trusted, much of which occurs when they are engaged. There is a huge body of research which shows that engaged employees perform better, tend to be healthier, and are more job satisfied. Harter and colleagues, in a major study, found that business units with employee engagement scores at the 99th percentile have nearly five times the success rate of those at the first percentile. Studies have also shown that actively disengaged employees miss more than six days of work per year, where engaged ones miss fewer than three days.

Fourth, take control of your own destiny and be engaged in change rather than oppose it. These have been themes that have come up time and time again. Indeed, it was Winston Churchill who once suggested that embracing change and encouraging it can help relieve stress:

> change is a master key. A man can wear out a particular part of his mind by continually using it and tiring it, just in the same way as he can wear out the elbows of his coats ... but the tired parts of the mind can be rested and strengthened, not merely by rest, but by using other parts ... it is only when new

cells are called into activity, when new stars become the lords of the ascendant, that relief, repose, refreshment are afforded.

And finally, "never have regrets." People who harbor resentment, missed opportunities and anger are those who have limited coping resources as they struggle with their inner turmoil.

chapter 19

Jeff Banks CBE – International Fashion Designer

Jeff Banks is an international designer of men's and women's clothing, jewellery and home furnishings. He founded his first boutique, called Clobber, in Blackheath, London, in 1964 and then the fashion chain Warehouse in 1976.

He holds honorary degrees from the University of Lancaster, East London, Newcastle, and Northumbria, University College for the Creative Arts, and the University of Westminster, and is a Doctor of Arts and a Doctor of Design. In 2009, Jeff was appointed as Commander of the Most Excellent Order of the British Empire in the Queen's Birthday Honours.

In 1964, with money saved from the paraffin business and from his father mortgaging the family home, Jeff opened Clobber, which carried his own designs along with other designers' work. It proved such a success that in 1969 he launched his own fashion label.

He opened his first standalone Jeff Banks shop in London, as well as retail outlets in 22 department stores, including Harrods and Harvey Nichols. In 1976, Jeff co-launched the fashion chain Warehouse, as well as continuing to work as a licensed designer. After it was taken over by retail chain Sears, he was sacked for being disruptive in board meetings – which he never regrets. In 1979 and 1981, he became British Designer of the Year, and in 1980 he was made "British Coat Designer of the Year."

His standing as a commercial force in retail fashion led to Jeff presenting over 320 episodes of "The Clothes Show," the BBC's long-running fashion show, which was broadcast on BBC One from 1986 to 2000. The show's success in gaining over ten million viewers led to the first "Clothes Show Live" event at the NEC in Birmingham, as well as the launch of the Clothes Show *magazine.*

Jeff continues to run his influential design studio in London's Soho and licenses his product in four countries through some 400 outlets. In 2011, Jeff began a joint venture of Jeff Banks retail shops in China and he now has 22 stores.

About Jeff

"I was born on 17 March 1943 in the Monmouthshire valley of Ebbw Vale in South Wales. My family moved to London when I was three years old. My father was a sheet metal worker who became a Trade Union leader and my mother came from a working class family in South Wales. My father left my mother when I was eight and I only ever saw him once again, when I was 11, but my mother and father reconciled when I was 17 and he moved back into the family home. Needless to say my relationship with my father in my formative years was somewhat lacking, but my mother and I became very close. She was largely unsupported by my father during these years and worked in the BHS café in Lewisham to support both me and her.

Neither of my parents were wealthy. After my father left my mother, I was offered a scholarship to an independent public school – St Dunstan's College, in Catford, South London. However, my mother couldn't afford the school uniform, so I went to Brockley County Grammar School instead. In order to afford the school uniform, I set up my own business, buying paraffin and delivering it at night on a barrow I made from pram wheels. I used to deliver the paraffin at night in five gallon drums to people who couldn't carry the fairly heavy fuel home.

By the time I was 13, I was earning almost ten times my mother's weekly wage and I bought an ex-army tanker and employed somebody to do the deliveries while I was at school. I sold the business when I was 15 and banked the money, which became part of my investment when I started up in business.

I was encouraged by a teacher to study art and realized that my art skills were limited during my first year at London's Camberwell School of Art, so transferred to studying interior design and latterly textiles at Central Saint Martin's College of Art and Design. I was quite academic at school, hence winning a scholarship, and became more enthusiastic about art as I matured through school. I eventually qualified with an art diploma, but couldn't get a job and ended up working for various design and display companies as a 3D artist.

A guy at my school at the age of 17 was bought a top of the range Austin Westminster car by his wealthy father. I decided I was never going to be last in the queue from that moment on. After leaving college, I was a freelance illustrator designing everything from fascias for supermarkets, to neons along Blackpool front, and interiors of bingo halls.

At the age of 21, I decided I was going to open an interior design office, and a friend of mine asked me if I'd like to go into business with him and open a small boutique. I thought I could open design offices upstairs from the shop and we could run the boutique almost as a sideline. On the first day we completely sold out. Then he and I decided that designing and retailing clothes was going to be our business.

I don't get stressed by business, as everything that happens during the course of the day is simply temporary that I don't go home at the end of each day and worry about. I am very fortunate that I run quite a large business with a very small dedicated team at its center, who all seem to enjoy what they are doing and function very well together.

The most challenging projects I have handled during my career were:

1. Making a film for the British Council at Expo 66 in Canada when I had neither directed nor produced a movie before, so that was a steep learning curve.

2. Starting up the world's first TV fashion program meant a lot of organizational time with the BBC and creating the original idea and seeing it through to fruition.
3. Creating 'Clothes Show Live', which became the fourth biggest exhibition in Britain, with 250,000 people going through the turnstiles in six days.

In terms of finding time to oversee and manage the various aspects of work – I just undertake what I think I can achieve during the day and only concentrate on things that I find pleasurable. I have a good team around me who work hard during the day. We tend not to work past 5:30 and rarely at weekends.

I don't particularly get stressed over anything, I just tend to get annoyed if people around me aren't performing to their best ability. Having made it clear what my expectations are, I tend to forget it and move on.

The recession has inevitably affected lots of businesses. Fortunately, my business has tended to go from strength to strength during the last five years, with a consistent increase in turnover in all the territories we operate. My one lesson from the recession is that you simply have to work harder and make your product and services better than the competition and pull everyone along with you in achieving that objective.

I think the six key points in being successful in business are:

1. Having a dream and vision.
2. Never being satisfied you have accomplished your dream.
3. Being honest and trustworthy.
4. Never being arrogant in thinking that nobody can do what you do.
5. Respecting every individual that works with you, no matter how low their job is.
6. Never losing sight of the fact that the customer is king.

Like most businessmen, I have learnt from successes and failures. An example of the latter: In 1974, a disgruntled individual who had an argument with one of my staff set fire to my business and, failing to settle the insurance claim, our bankers foreclosed and the business went into administration. This was exacerbated by the fact it was in the middle of the infamous three-day working week. I lost everything, including homes, cars, and all personal savings. After the administrator had taken the keys to the business off me, I went over to the pub to have a drink with the 100 staff to commiserate. One of my staff punched me in the face, blacked my eye, and knocked me out. When I came to I asked him why he had done that, as he was bigger than me and he said it was OK for me, as I would doubtless get started again, but for him it was his one chance of success. I have never treated anything that I do lightly after that moment, and it was a brutal lesson in accepting responsibility for everyone that works for you and not putting your own success in front of the just desserts of everybody else.

After this I moved into a small workroom in Camden Town with the help of one factory that had worked consistently for me and I managed to sign a licensing deal with a large Japanese company, who manufactured and marketed my product worldwide almost immediately. This proved to be the beginning of the beginning.

The fashion industry is a risk industry, but it is a question of evaluating the risk. I don't gamble purely on gut instinct because this could be to the detriment for not only myself but also the people that work for me.

When I look around, I don't think I have been particularly successful, as there are many other individuals that have made much more money in the textile industry then I could ever think of. I am, however, very lucky that after 50 years I am still doing the job that I love with lots of opportunities popping up all the time, and this has made me extremely happy, which I think is my measure of success: being happy, healthy, and a bit wiser then when I started out.

I am always extremely careful about budgeting and run a fairly tight ship without being overly extravagant. Everything I do has a priority which I tend to adhere to, as many people are dependent on my time which has to be carefully allocated. I am reasonably competent about expecting the unexpected and dealing with it.

I always believe in introducing new strategies that keep everybody on their toes, and I don't always test everything before proceeding, but I am always very careful not to undertake anything that could undermine the safety of the whole business.

I never get stuck in a rut and I am always reasonably adept at resolving situations that I get faced with. I don't run a cooperative; it's more like a soft dictatorship. I tend to analyze everything that I do. If I get feedback from various territories that I'm working with, or from market research that something isn't working, or is unacceptable, I go back to the drawing board and reconfigure.

I am constantly searching for new ideas and new initiatives that will improve our game and I am consistently working and pushing to improve quality standards. In essence, I am in the imagination business, and everyone with whom I deal with looks to me for the next big idea.

Timing is important in any business. Twenty-five years ago, I launched a concept called Good Goods, which to my knowledge is the truly first ethical clothing range. Cotton grown without pesticides or fertilizers, spun into yarns with a whole new technological background. Manufactured in Denmark in a state-of-the-art factory with the highest possible ethical standards for workforce compatibility and air conditioning to ensure no ingestion of any loose fibers. The garment dying process was strictly controlled to ensure that any water used was cleansed to drinking water standards at the end of the process. The whole manufacturing process was audited by David Bellamy Associates and it was a complete failure. Just way ahead of its time.

I don't think I am a workaholic because I enjoy everything I do, so it's not really a job. Sometimes, however, I exacerbate those people around me but I guess they have now learnt to live with it and just let me get on with it.

I really don't get stressed, but I am not averse to handing out the old Alex Ferguson hairdryer treatment every now and then. I don't really give advice to people on how to cope with stress because I am probably the stress maker. I guess one thing that I have learnt in life is that as long as nobody dies, it doesn't matter very much. If I were a doctor, fireman, policeman, or member of the armed forces I would really know what stress is and the responsibilities that go with it.

The principal qualities I look for in people who work for me are loyalty and complete honesty. I think after that a good sense of humor is absolutely vital. Those key ingredients and a good measure of ability help to cope with most things.

I am involved in the hiring and firing of staff, which is quite a rare occurrence, as most people seem to leave when their time with me is done. I have no regrets as I take pride in people moving on to greater and better things and would hope that their time with me proved to be a springboard for any future success.

I like to think that we work in a good, fun environment. It's not without its turbulent moments, but a good laugh at the end of the day always sets things up for tomorrow.

My advice to anybody going into business is to do something you are absolutely passionate about and never undertake something just for money.

The most important lesson I've learnt about business is that it's like a game of snakes and ladders. It has its ups and downs, and very often you end up back at the beginning, but when all is said and done, it's only a game."

ANALYSIS AND ADVICE

This is yet another example of someone who came from a deprived background, with an absent father for most of his formative years. It seems that for many successful people there is some loss-related event in early childhood which has influenced them in later life, providing them with "strength in adversity." Being able to deal with these adverse life events have helped them to cope later in life with less severe business issues, in other words providing them with "survival skills" and enabling them to contextualize the stresses and strains of business and to move on. A second issue is the ability to find something in life that one is passionate about.

Many of our interviewees have developed a passion about their work that makes them feel it is not actually work, but part of their life. As Sigmund Freud once wrote about psychology: "A man like me cannot live without a hobby-horse, a consuming passion – in Schiller's words a 'tyrant'. I have a tyrant, and in his service I know no limits. My tyrant is psychology." Levinson and Rosenthal in their book *CEO: Corporate Leadership in Action* suggested that "leadership; is a form of play" ... when one is in love with one's work, then the extraordinary hours are like play."

A third lesson is "accepting responsibility" personally for everyone who works with you. Most successful people achieve success with the help of others, and those who truly understand this are likely to experience sustainable rather than transitory success. This is partly related to being in touch with your past, particularly with your own past deprivations, and psychologically understanding what others you are working with might be feeling and needing. This can enable you to build effective working relationships, which is essential in almost any endeavor in life.

The fourth lesson is not being arrogant and believing your own press, or that "others couldn't do what you do." This is also about being rooted in reality rather than buying into the accolades and honors foisted on you in a successful career.

This interviewee summarizes it nicely by saying: "the most important lesson I've learnt about business is that it's like a game of snakes and ladders ... it has its ups and downs and very often you end up back at the beginning, but when all is said and done, it's only a game." This also implies being yourself, and being honest and trustworthy in your relationships.

And finally, the issue of being able to prioritize what is important and requires an immediate response and those that can be put on the "back burner" is a fundamental way of managing the stress of high-pressure jobs. The most effective copers seem to be able to decide what is needed to be done, and when to leave the overloaded "in tray" of minor issues alone.

20

Nigel Sillitoe – CEO, Insight Discovery, Dubai

Nigel Sillitoe is co-founder and, since 2009, CEO of Insight Discovery (ID), a Dubai-based strategic research company which specializes in stakeholder engagement (employees, customers, and investors) and leadership insights.

He has more than 25 years' experience in marketing, media communications, and sales. Prior to founding ID, Nigel set up the regional office of Mellon Bank in 2001, and subsequently developed that company as one of the most successful asset managers in the Middle East. Through ID, Nigel remains a high-profile speaker on the financial services conference circuit and is a regular contributor to publications such as International Adviser *and* MenaFM.

Many, but not all, of ID's existing clients are from the financial sector. A major focus going forward will be working across all sectors and industries to offer online employment engagement surveys, focus groups, and customer studies.

During 2012, ID was recognized as one of the top 50 service providers within the Middle East by MENA Fund Manager. In May 2013, ID received the award for Best Website (Services category) by the Pan Arab Web Awards Academy, and more recently Nigel was recently short-listed "Personality of the year" by Thomson Reuters.

About Nigel

"My early childhood was extremely happy, with plenty of outdoor activities in the surrounding area where we lived in Esher, Surrey. I was a hyperactive and rather mischievous child and was raised by my mother as my parents divorced when I was just four. The thing I remember most was being sent to boarding school at the age of seven. This wasn't, I should point out, because I was mischievous: both my sisters and brother also attended boarding schools from a young age. Being sent away from such a young age made a major impact on my life, in both a positive and negative way. It was positive in terms of making me incredibly independent. I also made some great friends, who I'm still in regular contact with. The big negative was that I didn't see much of my mother, which was emotionally tough at times. I was particularly close to mother, who raised four children by herself without any financial support from her ex-husband. Sadly, she died of cancer in her early 60s.

Both my parents were both comfortably well off and could be described as middle class. My father, Anthony Sillitoe, used to be Director of DeBeers, the security company, which my grandfather, Sir Percy Sillitoe, a former Director General of MI5, was an adviser to. Whilst my mother, Mary, rarely worked, she was incredibly enterprising, as she was an astute buyer and seller of property. Every two to three years, we moved house: the profit she made on these transactions helped to pay for all our private education. Her success was largely derived from always buying one of the smallest properties in the best areas. Typically, we would live in a central part of London like Chelsea, but always had the smallest mews house. My grandfather, on my mother's side, was entrepreneurial and also involved in property: from a very young age, he ran a successful building company, Derby & Co, which renovated houses bombed during World War II in the Bromley and Beckenham areas of South London.

Academically, I was pretty average. I scraped through with seven O Levels and one A level. My priority after school was to start work and earn money. Much later on in life, at the age of 30, I completed a two-year Open University diploma in management studies with Oxford

Polytechnic. I cannot ever remember being too hard up. This was probably because I wanted to be independent and earn money from a young age. I had holiday jobs from the age of 11. The very first job was arranged by a friend of my mother. I packed items in large containers for export at Allgood, an architectural ironmonger. Other jobs included sales at Oddbins, the liquor merchants, working at a pub on the King's Road in Chelsea, and being an accounts clerk for a Mercedes dealership. Most entertaining, in my late teens, was my job as a cocktail barman at La Valbonne. This was, at the time, one of London's leading nightclubs. All these holiday jobs made me realize that I enjoyed interacting with customers and working hard.

After I left school at the age of 18, a friend of my mother's introduced me to Minet, the Lloyd's broker. I was a reinsurance broker specializing in aviation. I found it incredibly dull – and very paper-driven, with most of the communicating with clients being done by telex. Within a year, I became – on a commission-only basis at the age of 20 – a financial adviser for Bishop Cavanagh in London. In the beginning, earnings were good but volatile. After two years, I began to wonder why I was in that line of business, given the high-pressure sales tactics and the fees on products, which were artfully hidden from customers.

I then joined Arbuthnot Latham, a London-based merchant bank. I was a trainee dealer in their unit trust operation. In essence, the job involved updating the unit prices of funds on whiteboards. Soon, I was promoted to being a broker salesman. This involved promoting Arbuthnot's products to financial advisers around the UK. It was then that I received my first company car, a Ford Escort, which I promptly wrote off within one month, when driving late at night, non-stop, from London to York.

This was followed by a series of investment fund sales jobs in and around the City of London at Brown Shipley, Framlington, James Capel Asset Management (which became HSBC Asset Management), NatWest, Barclays Global Investors, and Newton. The details varied from job to job. However, the big picture trend was this: I was often involved with green-field operations, which usually relied on developing new strategies and PR campaigns. My first real brush with the media was at NatWest. My first involvement with the Middle East and North Africa (MENA) region was with Newton and Mellon Bank (now The Bank of New York Mellon), which had acquired Newton.

I had the opportunity to move to Bahrain to set up a joint venture. My wife Helen, whom I married in 2001, moved to Bahrain that year. This was a particularly challenging time, because Helen was seven months pregnant and moving to a country she had never been to before. Then we had the tragic events of September 11, which took stress levels to a new high. Not only were we new parents, my first daughter having just been born in Bahrain, but I was also put under pressure to move everybody back to the UK. Luckily I persuaded Newton that I needed to stay put in order to conclude the joint venture. However, this was on the condition that we kept gas masks in our villa and taped all the windows.

From a business perspective, the first few years in Bahrain were hard. There weren't many institutional investors who were prepared to give mandates to a US-owned asset management group. With a bit of luck and lots of patience, within several years I had raised several billion dollars of capital for the various asset management companies owned by Mellon. I ran their small, but highly profitable, office in Bahrain for four years and then moved to Dubai in 2005, which coincided with the establishment of the Dubai International Financial Centre (DIFC). Given that Mellon was one of the first international companies to be overseen by the DFSA, the regulator of the DIFC, I was profiled in some DIFC advertising campaigns to try to attract other companies to move to the DIFC. This was fantastic free PR for both Mellon and myself! Over this time, Mellon became one of the most successful asset management companies in the MENA region: this was achieved by having a fantastic PA and three support staff based in London.

I was then tempted away to join London-based hedge fund company Thames River in 2007. Within two years of joining Thames River we had the global financial crisis, which resulted in the office in the DIFC being closed down. This was partly because of the lack of capital raised and partly because of the need to reduce costs. Being fired by my daughter's godfather, who was the CEO of Thames River, was difficult for both of us. Luckily this hasn't impacted our friendship.

I then thought long and hard about what I wanted to do next. Whilst there were opportunities to join another asset management company, I decided to take over the running of Menu Discovery, a small research house in which I was a shareholder. I had always wanted to run my own business. I also wanted to get away from the bureaucracy of large organizations – notwithstanding that I had been in charge of small and (fairly) autonomous operations in Dubai for Mellon.

The first thing that I did was to change the name of the company from Menu Discovery to Insight Discovery. In the past the company had focused on employee engagement surveys. However, given that my background was in the financial sector, I wanted to drive the business into new areas. Whilst my experience of market research at the time had been limited, I compensated this with my knowledge of marketing and media. I was also fortunate enough to meet Paul Gebara, a market research expert with experience at IPSOS Mori. He was the first senior colleague that I hired and he remains an external adviser.

The first couple of years of building the business was challenging. However, we have carved out a niche as the leading financial services research company covering the MENA region. We still do a significant amount of employee engagement surveys for MENA companies with offices spanning the globe. However, more of our revenue comes from bespoke research for international life insurance companies and international asset management companies. We are now in the process of expanding our services into Africa, which is an area of great interest to investors in the Middle East.

If I had to identify a career highlight, it would be the joint venture with the bank in Bahrain, as noted above. It took years to conclude. Negotiations were often in relation to very petty marketing rights. There was cultural conflict – not least because this was Mellon's first foray into MENA. We finally signed the contract which gave Mellon substantial assets to manage on behalf of major local institutions. The effort was worth it, because we would not have been able to win the business without the joint venture, short of spending years of effort.

I feel that I should also mention Insight Discovery's Middle East Investment Panorama (MEIP). This was a ground-breaking research report when we introduced it in 2009. It was the first systematic survey of international asset management companies and life insurers. It was satisfactory, but subsequent reports have been much better and this year we have attracted a record number of partners, which hopefully proves that we are delivering quality reports.

At about the same time, we won a mandate for research from Invesco, one of the world's leading international asset management companies. Whilst Invesco used our research, they hired another company to rewrite the actual report. In order to ensure that this problem would not recur, I engaged Andrew Hutchings as a consultant. He is a veteran financial analyst and commercial copywriter, who now serves as our Research Director. He transformed the way in which we report to our clients: indeed, I now believe that our report writing sets the benchmark for our peers in the MENA region.

In addition, I note that we are very careful about the business that we take on. As a result, we take on far fewer really challenging projects. For instance, hard experience has taught me that there are certain government-linked organizations who are difficult to do business with, due in particular to their very stringent procurement processes.

My CV shows that I am, by nature, someone who takes calculated risks. Further, most of my career has been spent in small organizations, or small outposts of large organizations. I have generally operated without a large infrastructure around me. Since launching Menu Discovery, I have had to build a business, but without the advantages of an established brand or a large balance sheet.

I realized early on that large organizations are usually bureaucratic in nature. Bureaucratic organizations never make decisions quickly. Often, slowness in decision-making means that opportunities get missed."

How do you cope with stress?

"I am impatient by nature and I find bureaucratic delays to be infuriatingly stressful. Living apart from my wife Helen and my daughters Francesca and Imogen is the other main source of stress. They moved back to the UK in 2010, mainly because of my daughters' schooling needs. Management of long-distance relationships requires a lot of discipline. I speak with my family almost every day via Skype. A visit to the gym is another important part of my daily routine.

Otherwise, I would suggest that a lot of things that would be very stressful to many other people don't bother me much at all. Our work is project-based. There are always many moving parts and multiple deadlines. I can cope with these – thanks in part to an app called Reqall, which is my memory-jogger. Work practices in the MENA region are very different to those of Western countries. Much more needs to be done by way of face-to-face meetings. Many employees are disempowered. The bottom line is that decision-making can be a cumbersome process. However, it goes with the territory. Clients in the region (including some governments) are slow payers. However, they are not non-payers. Cash flow planning is harder than in other parts of the world, but not impossible.

My career history is such that I have typically had few employees working with me. Whether my colleagues are employees or not, what really matters is that they are truly engaged with the enterprise. That is as true for Insight Discovery as it is for our clients. Within a large organization, it is imperative to assess how the employees feel, and what they think, in a systematic way. It is also very useful to know what the employees are like outside the work environment.

The nature of our business is such that I focus in a disciplined way on the relationships with senior colleagues – who are often consultants rather than employees in a formal sense. They are stakeholders whose passion and success are aligned with my own. By discussing the problems that I face with my senior colleagues – such as Andrew Hutchings – I can usually resolve them in a fraction of the time that it would take if I tried to deal with them myself.

If there was one piece of advice, besides the obvious one of being passionate about your business and services, it's continually striving to be innovative. You should enjoy every aspect of the business. You should have a stake – both financial and emotional – in the enterprise. You should feel energized to work for many years to come. Be pro-active, and remember that the client is always right.

More generally, I would suggest that successful careers come from both internal and external factors.

The internal factors relate to the way that you think about yourself and life in general. This will have a direct impact on the way in which you interact with actual and potential clients. People tend to buy goods and services from people that they like, especially if those people are passionate about what they do. It is also important that other elements of your life – family, health, and so on – are in balance and are aligned with your values and beliefs.

I would identify five factors that are external. Obviously, success comes from access to capital and from an understanding that cash flow and profit are not the same thing. Second, it is important to know what equity really is: it is the source of long-term value, and should not be given away. Third, business models should be scalable and saleable. Fourth, innovation is essential. You should always be able to look back to what you were doing two to three years ago and see very clearly that you are doing more things, doing different things, and/or doing them in smarter ways. Finally, you should always surround yourself with people who are better than you. If you stand on the shoulders of giants, you will see and travel further."

ANALYSIS AND ADVICE

Once again we can see that early childhood experiences like divorce are prevalent in the scenario of our successful business people. In addition, being sent off to boarding school at an early age is another life event of some significance. These kinds of events can have positive and negative effects on developing an individual's coping strategies later in life. Being at a boarding school can encourage self-reliance, independence, and sociability, which are worthwhile traits in later life, particularly in dealing with high-pressure jobs. Where it can be problematic is that it takes the child away from the stronger emotional ties to parents that many ordinary children can get from their parents, although this is not guaranteed in families.

One of the issues raised by this interview is how important it is for some people to be working in a smaller vs. a larger organization for them to feel in control, and avoid the stresses and strains of bureaucratic workplaces. Many of the problems in the workplace stem from cultures that are too bureaucratic or based on command and control, leaving innovative and creative businessman/women to either under-produce or suffer psychologically. We all need to find the right work environment and culture to thrive, and if there is a mismatch, stress will undoubtedly occur.

The second lesson we have taken from this is about the importance of a work/life balance fit. So many senior business people are working away from their families, which can have several negative consequences. First and most important is that the absent spouse/partner will not be engaging with their children and spouse; second, they may feel lonely; third, because they are away from the normal family demands, they will tend to work longer hours. None of these is good for family life or for the respective spouses/partners when they re-engage at the weekend.

Bebe Campbell Moore, in her book Successful Women, Angry Men, has suggested various ways in which couples who are frequently apart should cope: (a) setting aside time to talk in a relaxed way without interruptions; (b) try to communicate without being accusatory – e.g. "you come back after a week and don't do anything in the house"; (c) listen to the subtext of what the other is really saying; (d) don't try to solve all your issues or problems at once; and many more. It is about trying to communicate and resolve issues rather than getting drawn into endless rows.

And finally, make sure that you engage with your colleagues as much as possible face to face rather than through media. Relationship-building is essential as a precursor to effective communications, camaraderie, and high morale – all antidotes to workplace stress.

chapter 21

Sally Gunnell OBE – Former British Olympic Champion

Sally Gunnell started athletics life as a pentathlete and long jumper with the Essex Ladies' club. Gold at the Edinburgh Commonwealth Games of 1986 seemed to confirm Sally's prowess at sprint hurdling, and in 1989, she took gold at the European Cup 400m flat race in Gateshead. By 1990, she was successfully hurdling again and won the 1990 Commonwealth Games 400m hurdles title in Auckland.

Tokyo's 1991 World Championships could so easily have brought Sally the gold medal; however, in the lead at the penultimate hurdle, she glanced across at one of her rivals. That uncharacteristic split second of mental diversion left her with the silver and a burning sense of disappointment. She returned to the track's biggest stage in 1992: the Barcelona Olympics, where she progressed to the 400m hurdles final and an Olympic gold and a place in history were hers.

Sally worked even harder during the off-season of 1992/3 to get in peak condition for the World Championships in Stuttgart, where despite feeling well below par, she stormed to the gold, setting a new world record in the process.

Although her later career was blighted by injury, eventually coming to an end in 1997, Sally's achievements in '92 and '93 assured her place in the history books. No other woman has held Commonwealth, European,

World, and Olympic track titles concurrently and her Stuttgart time remains a British record.

Sally became part of the BBC Sport team and was a regular fixture on athletics programs throughout the 90s until 2006, interviewing athletes and bringing the trackside atmosphere to millions of living rooms across the UK. She has appeared in numerous TV shows, including "A Question of Sport," and is a regular on TV breakfast shows as well as on radio. Sally's corporate work, helping companies to bring health and well-being into the workplace, confirm her formidable reputation as an influencer at the highest levels of business.

About Sally

"My mission today is to promote health and well-being for everybody in the UK. I am a passionate supporter of initiatives that encourage families to be more active.

I grew up on a farm in Chigwell, Essex, and my parents were both working class. A lot of my life was spent outdoors and I was very active from a young age and spent a lot of time outside running around and riding my bike. I didn't join an athletics club until I was about 12; however, I was very sporty. You would always find me running about outside and doing cartwheels. My parents were sporty at school and had a very good work ethos. They were always busy running the farm. I used to get up at 5 a.m. every morning, the same time as my Dad, and help milk the cows and other jobs round the farm. Mum was very much head of the house, cooking the meals, and getting everything ready. I have two older brothers. Although they enjoyed sport at school, they didn't end up being athletes.

I left school knowing that I wanted to make a living out of my running. I had the support of my parents rather than getting a job or going on and doing further education. My ambition to be a full-time athlete was a big gamble. I used to train twice a day and wrote loads of sponsorship letters, and applied for grants from different areas. The motivation was for achievement, never money, and what I could physically achieve on the sporting field.

I wasn't particularly academic. I struggled at school and running was my life from the age of 14. When I was about 16, I decided that it would be easier to pursue my ambition to run as a career if I stayed on at sixth form.

My first job when I left school was working part-time in a restaurant/bar, which allowed me to train in the morning, work at lunchtime, then train again in the afternoon. After that, I worked as a nanny looking after two little boys, and the parents were very good at being flexible around my training. I then got a sponsorship deal with an accountancy firm. I was with them for six years, working in the research department twice a week, and received the basic wage which allowed me to train.

These days people have much more of a chance to do the academic side and engage in whatever sport they're interested in through their college or university and get all the support they need - I had to choose one or the other. I look back now and think I was very lucky for it to have worked out, because if I had got a silver medal, it wouldn't have been the same and I wouldn't have made a living out of it. Back in those days, it was for me the sheer enjoyment and challenge of what I was doing and I never looked further than that.

The proudest moments in my career were winning a gold medal in the Olympics. It's the pinnacle for any sports person in the athletics world. That's what you dreamed about since you were little, and it's the main achievement. Also, getting an OBE is a wow factor. I'm very proud of that achievement, as well as having three lovely children – Finley 15, Luca 12, and Marley 8."

How do you cope with stress?

"In terms of coping with stress before a big event, I have learnt to block out all negative thoughts and ensure that all the preparation was done, so I had no excuses to do badly on the day. You only get a very small window to get it right and you have to believe in your own capability.

I used to do a lot of visualization and mental preparation a year in advance and would think about the race and what I had to do. Sometimes I thought about it 30 times a day. It was about mentally taking yourself to that race and believing that you were capable of doing it and that you were as good as everyone else.

I have had a lot of injuries during my career. After three really good years, I started to get various injuries like Achilles tendon, which is all part of being an athlete. As soon as I worked that out in my mind, that was the turning point in my career. One of my worst injuries in 1995, (bone spur behind the Achilles tendon) resulted in me having to have an operation, then 12 months to recover. It came after the high points in my career, and when I look back now it wasn't the end, even though it seemed like it at the time.

After doing a lot of running and motivation speeches, I realized how much exercise and nutrition can affect who you are as a person. Dealing with stress comes down to what you eat and the exercise you do. Both can play a major part. I set up Sally Gunnell Healthy Living (www.sallygunnell.com) about three years ago. Our mission is to promote health and well-being for everyone in the UK, mainly through corporate work. Everyone is under pressure these days, and often doing two people's work. My team of experts (which includes nutritionists, sports therapist, and fitness expert) show clients how to cope with stress through a special program of diet and exercise.

I would say the key point of being successful in life is knowing what you want to achieve. Having goals is important so that you know where you want to be in a year or six years' time. It's also important to have a good support team around you, rather than trying to do everything on your own. Other important factors: be yourself and try not to be someone you're not. Set new challenges and don't be scared of changing and moving on to something else. I think my success story is that I have managed to keep going for this number of years, especially when you hear of so many companies going out of business.

I have learnt massively from successes and failures. Never dwell on failures. Try to put them behind you as quickly as possible. Everyone has setbacks in business. One of the hardest things when I retired from athletics 15 years ago was judging people and knowing who to trust. That's probably one of the biggest lessons in business.

My husband Jonathan and I have invested quite a lot in property. We are not big risk takers and rely mainly on good advice and gut instinct. If we aren't 100% sure about something, we don't go ahead with it. Having experienced setbacks in the past, we are cautious about everything we do these days. We like to spread our investments to limit the risk and have an emergency pot to enable us to get hold of money quickly if something goes wrong. We would never invest in one area that we couldn't touch for 10–20 years. I realize that anything could happen at any point in time, so I am very cautious.

I like to prioritize on a daily basis and I am a real 'list' person. I like to have a certain amount of achievements each day, which is important for me. If something unexpected comes along, I like to deal with it straight away rather than putting it off until later.

As far as implementing changes on the work front, we are always trying to do new things and trying to find out what works and what doesn't. If we introduce something new, we ensure that it's adaptable to every company and person we work with to ensure success. You learn by your mistakes, and if it's not going the way you want, just move on. I learnt that as an athlete and the same is true about business. If I'm stuck in a rut, I go for a walk or run, as it makes everything a lot clearer.

I think it's important to have a good team around you – it's no different from when I was running. We are constantly striving to help as many people as we can with their health and well-being and using our knowledge of the health and nutritional market to make work more enjoyable for everyone.

The number of hours I work varies as I do so many different things. I realize the quality time with my children is very important so I factor that in and try to get the right balance. I don't have a structured nine to five day.

Exercise is extremely important, even if it's only going for a walk or 20 minutes of sit-ups or yoga. It not only keeps your heart healthy but releases endorphins, which help combat stress. It's an important message that I like to get across to people.

We all have days when it feels like everything is against you. When it happens to me, I put everything down and go outside for a 20 minute run or go and work out in the gym. Everyone suffers with stress and it's important to know how to cope with it. The situations that cause me the most stress are deadlines or things that have gone wrong at home or at work. I am no different from anyone else and worry about them; however, I realize that if I go for a run I will be able to deal with it better and have a clearer understanding of the situation.

The qualities that I look for from people that I work with are enthusiasm and dedication. I also employ people that I feel comfortable with, which is equally important. I set targets for them and reward incentives at the end of the year to people who have worked hard to show our appreciation. I believe a good sense of humor relieves stress and a few jokes don't go amiss.

The most important thing I have learnt about life is how powerful your mind is. Have belief in yourself and you will achieve it. I would do everything the same way again, if I started from scratch."

ANALYSIS AND ADVICE

If you are an athlete, it is important to ensure you have proper nutrition and exercise. They are fundamental to performance, but they are also central to a stress management and coping strategy for most of us in high-pressure jobs. As Palmer and Cooper contend in their book *How to Deal with Stress*: "There are many benefits from taking exercise. These include improving your physical and mental health, stress busting, anger control, weight control, reducing depression, and enhancing self-esteem. For many people, exercise works by distracting them from their difficulties and problems...."

A second learning lesson is "being realistic about achieving your dreams." Many people suffer from stress by having unrealistic expectations about what they would like to achieve, and experience the stress associated with disappointment. This disappointment gets personalized into "I'm not good enough to do that," "I'm a failure," which can severely damage one's self-esteem and make them vulnerable to any excessive pressure at work or in their personal life.

Third, it is vital for people living and working in high-pressure environments to "never dwell on failures." People who relive "what could have been" will never cope well with the "here and now," and could damage their ability to be adaptable and resilient.

The fourth lesson is about mental preparation and visualiza-tion, the latter of which has helped many athletes to focus on their immediate goals and imagine how they might win a race or competition. There is a great deal of psychology on "cop-ing imagery," where an individual imagines or visualizes what might happen when you are doing a major presentation at work or going for an important job interview. What you need to do is run through various scenarios of a potential stressful event. Palmer and Cooper suggest a five step process: Step 1 – Think about the situation you are stressed about; Step 2 – Note down the aspects of the situation that you are stressed about; Step 3 – Develop ways to deal with these; Step 4 – Visualize yourself in that situation, and slowly picture yourself coping with each anticipated difficulty that arises, repeating this four or five times; Step 5 – Practice this again whenever you are confronted by the same situation.

And finally, be yourself and try not to be someone you're not. Set new challenges and don't be scared of changing and moving onto something else. These two points are fundamental to lay-ing the groundwork for an effective personal coping strategy. As Winston Churchill once wrote:

> Many remedies are suggested for the avoidance of worry and mental overstrain by persons who, over prolonged periods,

have to bear exceptional responsibilities and discharge duties upon a very large scale. Some advise exercise, and others, repose. Some counsel travel, and others, retreat. Some praise solitude, and others, gaiety. No doubt all these may play their part according to the individual temperament. But the element which is constant and common in all of them is change.

chapter 22

Ann Pickering – Human Resources Director, Telefónica UK

Ann Pickering joined O2 in 2004 to head up the HR team in Customer Services and was appointed to the UK Board in 2008.

Prior to joining O2, Ann worked for Marks and Spencer, Fidelity, and Xansa (now Steria). She is a chartered Fellow of the Institute of Personnel Development.

These previous roles enabled Ann to gain experience in creating and implementing key strategic developments from an HR perspective in both the UK and abroad, including a joint venture in the banking industry and integrating HR cultures and competencies with a newly acquired IT company in India.

Since joining O2, Ann has seen the company achieve a top 20 place three times in the Sunday Times Top 100 Employers in the UK and eighth place in the UK Best Places to Work in 2012. Outside O2, Ann is a Board member of the "Unlock the Cure" Appeal, part of the Breast Cancer Charity formed specifically to focus on unlocking the cure for breast cancer. She has also recently been appointed as an Advisory Board member of Sheffield University Business School.

About Ann

"I grew up in Liverpool and was one of six children. My dad was the son of an Irish farmer and my mum the daughter of an Irish publican. I also attended a Convent Grammar school, so it was a very traditional Irish Catholic upbringing.

My parents weren't wealthy. Having six children is a tough gig! My father supplemented his income with evening jobs to help make ends meet. When my mother was 40, she decided that she wanted to go to university. Her decision had a huge impact on family life. On the one hand I was angry, as she was 'different' from other mothers, but I later realized that this decision and everything else she did instilled into her five daughters an unfailing sense of self-belief. She also taught me the importance of not being afraid to try something new.

I look back at my childhood and realize that as a family we were very hard up. For example, all six of us had free school meals. But both my parents worked incredibly hard to ensure we always had what was needed, and this had a huge impression on me as I began my working life. I have always believed hard work is important, and I'm sure this is because my parents instilled this attitude in me from a young age.

I was reasonably bright, but to be honest I was more interested in sport than being academic. However, I did well enough to read English at London University. I was appointed Head Girl whilst at school. This was my first experience of leadership and I loved it! I learnt how to represent the views of my colleagues to the teaching staff and vice versa; a skill that has stood me in good stead throughout my career, especially when it came to employee relations. Also growing up in Liverpool ensures you never become cocky, and that authenticity is important.

During my university holidays I worked at M&S in Liverpool. The job gave me the opportunity to experience a variety of different roles, working with diverse teams, and customers. The experience really helped shape my thoughts about what I wanted out of my career.

I really decided what career I wanted to pursue when I was a student working at Marks and Spencer. My experience taught me that I wanted to work with other people, in a leadership role, and for a company that would offer me variety. I applied to the M&S HR graduate training scheme and was successful … I guess you could say the rest is history!

As the HR Director for Telefónica UK my responsibilities are often widespread and varied. And with this breadth and variety comes high volume. An ability to balance my workload is therefore critical. I apply a laser-like focus, concentrating on the things that will make a difference to the business, rather than the 'nice to haves'. I also need to keep abreast of the latest technology. For example, we launched 4G in 2013 and as the technology becomes available nationwide it has the potential to transform mainstream services, making life that little bit easier.

One of my most challenging projects was when, in the late 1980s, I worked in financial services in the city and had to implement a major redundancy exercise. This was my first experience of such an initiative and it taught me the importance of treating people with dignity and respect. Whilst at Xansa, I was part of the M&A team that acquired an offshore IT house in India, again a first for me. Finally, in O2, opening a call center from scratch in Glasgow was a huge challenge – finding suitable premises, recruiting, and training a thousand employees and even choosing an O2 tartan!"

How do you cope with stress?

"I am ruthless about my work/life balance. I try to take exercise at least three times a week and spend as much time with my family as possible. I also try to laugh every day … it's a great stress buster.

Finding time to oversee and manage the various aspects of the work is largely due to my team, who manage the day-to-day aspects on my behalf. You can be the best leader in the world, but if you don't have a capable team supporting you, you will fail.

I also rely on being able to work flexibly – both in and away from the office. At O2 we've pioneered flexible working practices for quite some time. As someone who lives in Sheffield but works in Slough, having the freedom and tools to work flexibly can make all the difference.

Managing stress: for me there are three key factors:

- Firstly, ensure that you have a team of people working with you with the skills and experience you need to ensure projects run as smoothly as they can.
- Secondly, it's important to prioritize your own work/life balance – whether that's exercising, spending time with family, or trying out something new. Maintaining a good work/life balance is vital in reducing stress.
- Finally, it's critical to always keep a sense of perspective in whatever you do.

While there's no hard and fast rule for being successful in business, my top tips would be:

1. Be proactive – make sure that you apply a 'can-do' attitude to everything that you do.
2. Hire the right talent – invest time in employing people with the right skills and attitude.
3. Realize that it's a team effort – you can't achieve success on your own.
4. Be willing to learn from others – whether that's young people coming into your business or people who have been there for years – you're never too old to learn.
5. Think outside the box – seek inspiration from a wide variety of places – whether that's volunteering with a local community group, at work, or at home.
6. Be persistent! If you believe in what you are doing you have to fight for it – no one else will.

The main thing I've learnt is that emotional resilience is essential if you are to become a senior leader in business. Sometimes you need to make bold, tough, commercial decisions and it's important that you can do this with a level head.

Secondly, as your career progresses, how you achieve things becomes more important than what you achieve. You need to take on more of a leadership role and be less 'hands on', so the ability to lead and motivate becomes vital.

HR is all about people, and, by their very nature, people are unpredictable. This means that for me, gut instinct plays an important part in my world. But, there's no substitute for information and data. When you're in a leadership position decisions must be based on insight and data as well as intuition."

What is your biggest business success to date?

"There have been a few that I'm particularly proud of. When I worked at Xansa, I was part of the team that led the acquisition of an Indian software company. This was one of the first offshore acquisitions in our industry and was particularly ground-breaking at the time.

At O2, there have been several moments. I was instrumental in the development of a brand new call center in Glasgow. We created the center from scratch, so it felt like a particular achievement when it was up and running. O2 has also appeared several times in the Top 20 Best Companies to Work For – a great moment for an HR Director.

While I set a 'To Do' list for the week, in reality I have to prioritize daily as something unexpected often arises, meaning that my well-intended plans go awry. The key is to remain flexible at all times and focus ruthlessly on what will make the most difference to the business.

In the digital world that I work in, you have to be agile as it's constantly evolving; for example, the way I communicate with my team has changed. I often use Yammer, and regularly run my meetings remotely using Lync.

I believe it's really important to be able to juggle ambiguity and come to your own conclusions. There's usually more than one right answer to every problem so I try to find time to talk to people both inside and outside the business and seek inspiration from colleagues, friends, and family at all levels.

At O2, we're bringing hundreds of young people into our business every year via our internship, apprenticeship, and graduate schemes. As the generation to have grown up with the Internet, they have swathes of skills that many other generations don't – our recent Telefónica Millennials Survey, for example, showed that almost half of young people in the UK say that they have an excellent knowledge of technology. I make sure that I involve these bright, young people in my work to help bring a fresh perspective to a problem or challenge.

Finally, I make sure that I keep up-to-date with current affairs. I read a daily newspaper as well as key HR journals to ensure that I'm aware of all the latest industry developments.

At O2, we LOVE trying out new ideas – that's what made us so successful! There's no such thing as a negative reaction, only feedback; you must take it and learn from it.

Both my parents believed in the power of hard work, so I do like to stretch my teams to achieve results. Timing is critical in business, but that doesn't always mean doing things first. A company can be a 'fast follower' and be hugely successful. Flexibility is also key, learn fast (or indeed fail fast) and move on. A rigid approach in business seldom works.

I have learnt to cope with stress over the years, partly because I believe most people are inherently good, so if I can't work someone out, it really perplexes me. I'm lucky to work for a company that has strong values and looks after its customers and its employees, which allows me to sleep well at night.

My main piece of advice to anyone suffering from stress is to retain a sense of perspective. As long as you're confident that you've truly tried your best, that's all you can do.

One of the main qualities I look for from people who work with me is that they have the right attitude. While there is no doubt that technical ability is important, you can teach someone new skills, but you can't teach someone a different attitude.

At O2, we have a huge focus on talent development, concentrating on how we can nurture and upskill those working for us. This often means bringing bright young minds into our business who might not have the experience just yet, but who have the attitude and desire to succeed. These are the kinds of people I want on my team.

I spend a considerable amount of time recruiting people and at times I need to dismiss people also. If these people go on to achieve success in another company, that's a positive thing.

I believe that laughter can be a great stress reliever. When you spend a lot of time with people in a work environment, it's incredibly important to have fun with your colleagues, as well as just working hard.

My advice to enterprising businessmen and women: be proactive, be energetic, and be curious. Seek inspiration from everything you do, whether that's volunteering with a local community group, at work, or from friends and family. And most importantly, have fun!

The most important lesson I've learnt is that there is nothing more important than your health. Ultimately, you have to look after yourself if you are to succeed in business and in life."

ANALYSIS AND ADVICE

There are a range of tips for managing stress that this HR Director has suggested. First, put everything that happens to you at work and in life in some kind of perspective. You can do this by a psychological coping strategy called "constructive self talk". That means that you say to yourself, "my budget at work has been cut, or some key person is leaving, or one of my staff has been angry at me, and I am very upset, but this event is not life- or even job-threatening." As Palmer and Cooper suggest in their book How to Deal with Stress, you need to de-magnify or "de-awfulize" the event, because otherwise you will blow it out of proportion, which can have serious health consequences:

> events may be difficult to deal with, or even be plain bad, but are they really "the end of the world," "horrendous," "awful," "horrible"? Seldom are events we face on a day-to-day basis that bad. To examine stress scenarios dispassionately, we recommend that you distance yourself from your immediate stress-inducing thinking to help you "see the wood for the trees."

The second lesson is about being ruthless about making sure you have good work/life balance. You need to switch off from your work-related problems when you get home. This could be achieved by not accessing your computer or smartphone to pick up emails, and ensuring that you spend good quality time with your family and friends. This also means taking exercise and investing in your few good friends by ensuring you are seeing them on a regular basis. Doing things for other people outside of work, whether charitable or in the community, can inoculate you from the stresses of your job.

The third issue, which has been touched on by several interviewees, is the "importance of treating people with dignity and respect," and how in the longer term this can prevent stress at work because the major source of excessive pressure comes from our relationships with others. Even well-known fiction authors have recognized the significance of relationships in the workplace. The main character in Joseph Heller's book *Something Happened* reflected on his relationships at work:

> In the office in which I work there are five people of whom I am afraid. Each of these five people is afraid of four people (excluding overlaps), for a total of twenty, and each of these twenty people is afraid of six people, making a total of one hundred and twenty people who are feared by at least one person.

He goes on to say in terms of his immediate team "there are six people who are afraid of me and one small secretary who is afraid of all of us. I have one other person working for me who is not afraid of any, not even me, and I would fire him quickly, but I'm afraid of him." Although a humorous portrayal, many of the sentiments should strike a psychological chord with many of you.

And finally, it is important that individuals develop "emotional resilience," where they bounce back from challenges and setbacks and can use their coping resources to get up, dust themselves off and take on the next challenge.

chapter 23

Lord Karan Bilimoria CBE, DL – Co-founder and Chairman, Cobra Beer

In 2006, Karan Bilimoria was appointed Lord Bilimoria of Chelsea, making him the first ever Zoroastrian Parsi to sit in the House of Lords. Lord Bilimoria was the Founding President of the UK India Business Council, former Deputy President of the London Chamber of Commerce and Industry, a former Chancellor of Thames Valley University (and the youngest ever university chancellor at the time of appointment at one of Britain's largest universities), and he is a Deputy Lieutenant of Greater London.

He has served on the Government's National Employment Panel, and was Chairman of the Panel's Small and Medium Enterprise Board from 2001 to 2005. Lord Bilimoria is the founder of Cobra Beer, and Chairman of the Cobra Beer Partnership Limited, which for many years has been one of the fastest growing beer brands in the UK. In 2004 he was awarded the Commander of the British Empire (CBE); then in 2008 he was awarded the Pravasi Bharatiya Samman by the President of India, the highest honor given to members of the 30 million-strong Indian diaspora across the world.

About Karan

"I was brought up with two primary influences; one being military, as my father was Commander in Chief of the Central Indian Army, and the other being business, which came from my mother's side where my great grand-father was a leading entrepreneur in the city of Hyderabad, serving also as a member of the Upper House of the Indian Parliament. Both aspects instilled values and ethics from a very young age which I still live by to this day, chief among which is a profound sense of integrity.

I come from a family of high achievers so there were expectations on me to strive to achieve as others had done before me. I was also inspired to emulate their success. The English education system also had a big influence on my early life, as I am the third generation of my family to be educated in England, which I believe gives you a very good start in life, and gives you skills that encourages competitiveness and a willingness to succeed; essential attributes in business.

My career to date has been very rewarding and enjoyable. However, as a leader and employer there is pressure. The main pressure comes from the fact that the buck stops with you. The business is driven by you and it's not an easy journey – there are going to be bumps on the road. It is the ability to survive and see it through which is the important thing.

Raising finances is very difficult for any fledgling business. Once the business has taken off everything becomes much more controllable. Establishing your brand is the biggest challenge and it doesn't come without an iron will and absolute dedication. With Cobra, I am not satisfied with 10% to 12% growth. I want to grow at more than double that rate – this is what drives me, the desire to push and not to be satisfied with 'good' results when they could be 'great'!

If business is failing, entrepreneurs and business people in general need to quickly identify exactly what is failing them, then do everything in their power to resolve the problem. You also need to realize if the situation is hopeless and to understand when it's time to walk away."

How do you cope with stress?

"My role is at its most stressful when I feel I cannot fit everything into a day. Constantly prioritizing my time can be very stressful, but with a good team to help me it's possible to get everything done. A good way to cope with stress is to always leave your desk clean at the end of each day. It's something my father taught me – it helps clear your mind before you go home so you don't take work worries into your personal life. The key to coping with the stresses of business is knowing where to draw the line and consistently enforcing this. Family time must always come first.

I have a saying that we hire for 'will rather than skill'. That's not to say our people are not skilful, but that they must first have the right attitude: a willingness to learn. It's also important to give people the freedom to achieve and enjoy the satisfaction from their achievements. Treat people well and they will become your strongest assets in tough times as you will have instilled loyalty and a feeling of partnership. I have never regretted letting anyone go – we have lost very few people over the years and I can honestly say that whenever a person has moved on, it has been the right decision for them and the business.

I have a motto in business –'adapt or die'. You must accept and prepare for the unexpected and to do this you must adapt in response to the unexpected.

My strengths include the ability to innovate and be creative. Looking ahead and anticipating the next thing has stood me in good stead. Another skill I've been able to develop is being able to manage a variety of people and stakeholders.

My weaknesses include trying to do too much in a day. I've learnt that it's impossible to do everything. In my early days I was also guilty of focusing on high growth at the expense of profitability. Since then I've been able to strike a balance between the two."

ANALYSIS AND ADVICE

The concept of "fitting everything into a day" continually comes up as a theme among our high-pressure interviewees. There is a need to prioritize all that lands on their proverbial desk. Palmer and Cooper, in *How to Deal with Stress*, come up with a list of seven behaviors that might help. First, at the beginning of each day make a list of all the things you need to do and prioritize that list and get those done. You can hold over lower priority goals for another day. Second, avoid procrastinating: it is too easy to avoid doing the difficult or more complex tasks. Third, to avoid errors of judgment or mistakes, try to do one thing at a time. Fourth, allow time for the unexpected, and be realistic about how much work you and your colleagues can do. Fifth, avoid automatically saying 'yes' to others' requests, which means learning to say 'no' to low-priority requests. Sixth, when you receive post or emails, prioritize them rather than answering immediately ... those that are not very important, either politely say you can't do them or put them down the list for another day or week.

Seventh, do all your outgoing calls in priority order, like your post or emails. While doing complex or intensive work, divert your phone and close your computer.

Another interesting suggestion here is to clear your work priorities for each day, so that your overload doesn't spill over into your private life. To be effective in coping with stress, we all need time away from the pressure points to invest in our families and close personal friends. The Roman Emperor Marcus Aurelius, in AD 161, once wrote "you participate in a society by your existence. Then participate in its life through your actions – all your actions. Any action not directly toward a social end (in this case being part of a family) is a disturbance to your life, an obstacle to wholeness, a source of dissension." And as we hear from this interviewee, "family time must always come first."

A third lesson we can learn has to do with who you work with and the notion of "will rather than skill," that is, recruiting and working with people with the right attitude, with a willingness to learn is important in creating a stress-free "people conflict" culture. Find compatible people to work with, treating them with respect and trust, and you are at least half way to creating a more livable culture.

And finally, making sure your actions are based on a sense of integrity. The more an individual is true to him/herself the less they will be stressed by others' perceptions, as Marcus Aurelius once wrote:

> it never ceases to amaze me: we all love ourselves more than other people, but care more about their opinion than our own. If a god appeared to us – or a wise human being, even prohibited us from concealing our thoughts or imagining anything without immediately shouting it out, we wouldn't make it through a single day. That's how much we value other people's opinions – instead of our own.

Conclusion

We hope that this book has not only given you greater insight into the stresses and strains on high-pressure people, but also on how they tend to deal with it in their busy lives – whether it's a stressful situation at work, a life-changing decision, or a personal issue at home.

Stress is something we can't avoid. However, we can limit its impact by introducing stress management techniques into our daily lives. We hope our interviewees have provided you with some interesting pressure management tips. Some stress, or should we say pressure, can be positive, but you need to find the level that's right for you. Coping with stress is personal to each individual, like taking exercise, having a power nap at lunchtime, or doing deep breathing exercises.

It's apparent from the interviews that we've carried out that most of our interviewees were motivated from an early age to do well in life via a combination of determination, energy, and drive. This served each interviewee well in their future careers and helped them to get where they are today. Another common pattern emerging from the 23 interviews we carried out was that each interviewee possessed communication, leadership, and management skills, and had the ability to recognize and manage stress at different levels.

Our overall analysis found some common themes:

Early childhood experience. We believe that early childhood experience is a significant element, particularly in the formation of our interviewees' basic attitudes and their perception of themselves *vis-à-vis* the world.

Childhood, for many of our interviewees, was in the psychological sense a period of insecurity and loss. This led to a subsequent drive and need to control their own future.

Value and belief system. Each person we interviewed had a well-developed value and belief system. While these varied from individual to individual, this key element gave each a clarity of vision and purpose.

Responsibility. An important element was that each of our interviewees had taken on a high degree of responsibility at an early age. This allowed them to develop managerial and executive skills they would need later on in their careers.

Leadership. Leadership style and personal charisma were common to all our interviewees. This element of charismatic leadership provides both drive and direction to the organizations they work for.

Communication. The ability to communicate was another element that each of our interviewees possessed, particularly the ability to allow themselves to be open and honest about their feelings and attitudes.

So what are the key issues we have learnt from our analysis of the various interviews we've carried out?

- That deprivation and failure can be the precursors for success. It has been found in numerous studies that experiencing loss or deprivation can motivate individuals to achieve and gain control of a world later in life that they were unable to control when they were younger.
- Take control of events, rather than letting them control you. A great deal of psychological research has found that people who take control and look for options to deal with problems are the ones who cope better and have least negative outcomes. Find people in the work environment you can "let off steam" with. By externalizing your worries to others, they can help you find solutions before the problem becomes either serious or terminal.
- That the fear of failure can also be a good motivator and enable the individual to learn new and more resilient coping strategies.
- Be flexible. In order to cope with all the stresses and strains of pressured jobs, we need to adapt to everything that is thrown at us in the workplace and in life. We need to get away from a rigid mentality

and behavioral set, epitomized by this humorous quote from Samuel Goldwyn "I'm willing to admit that I may not always be right, but I am never wrong."

- Have space to reflect on those things that trouble us, some "peaceful space" to reflect on how we should deal with an issue, rather than just reacting emotionally immediately.
- Share your concerns with someone you trust, whether a partner/ spouse, close friend, or family member. Keeping problems repressed is an unhealthy coping strategy. This is closely allied to seeking social support if you need it, rather than trying to be macho man/woman. It is all too easy in business to hide your problems behind a veneer of self-confidence, a problem which in the end can eat away at you and cause serious health problems.
- Do those everyday things that make you relax and unwind for a short time – what we call "recovery activities" such as swimming, listening to music, relaxation exercises, or taking a walk. Churchill found solace during the war in painting, as a way of taking time out from the multiple demands and long hours.
- Identify what underlies your "stress reaction" before looking at the options to deal with it. If you are feeling anxious or depressed, what is causing it at work, and what are the various options of dealing with it?
- Have a sense of purpose, a vision, and passion, and don't divert from it.
- Stay rooted. Don't believe your own press and never get too big to be told of problems at work or to be open to other people's constructive criticisms. This is easily done as a person moves up the success hierarchy.
- Never look back and say "I wish I had" or "I should have." Learn from your mistakes but don't dwell on them. The people who get ahead in life are those that have a "bounce-back" mentality. "I have failed, I will learn from this" then get on with the next venture without wallowing in the failure.
- Contextualize all your worries and ask yourself: "Is this life-threatening?." If not, try to find a solution to it that is as rational and as analytical as possible.
- Trying to change something in your workplace or in society is extremely difficult, so concentrate on those things you can change.

- Given that life is a one-act play, do as Frederick Forsyth suggests, and give it "your best shot – if it works you're lucky and if it doesn't don't let it destroy you." Again we need to learn from failure and not embrace it!
- It is vital to have a good working relationship with your colleagues, and to treat them fairly because, down the line, they can be your social support system when you need it either at work or personally.
- It is important to be able to prioritize your work and other aspects of your life. Stress occurs frequently when people fail to deal with the important things in their lives or work, and let the less pressing or "easy to do" stuff to take priority – usually because these are less complex, or involve less emotionality, or are less painful to do.
- In dealing with what appear to be insolvable problems, it is best to break them down into smaller solvable parts, which provides you with the self-confidence to deal with the bigger picture further down the line.
- Make sure you are in a job you love, that provides you with purpose, or as Confucius reflected "choose a job that you like and you will not have to work a day in your life."
- Stay away from "glass have empty" people. They are a drain on your emotional resources and a major source of stress.
- Create a team around you that provides the social support you need to do your job, and who you can turn to when times get tough, as we have seen over the last seven years of the recession.
- Tensions that build up in the workplace or even in the home can frequently be temporarily relieved by humor, so that the underlying tensions can eventually be brought to the surface and dealt with. Humor not only relieves tension, but also creates an atmosphere where people, in a less than confrontational way, can talk more informally about their problems.
- Be flexible – it's a coping strategy that unlocks problems rather than exacerbates them.
- Have passion for what you do. This means that you and the people around you will enjoy the nine to five rather than tolerate it.
- Prioritize your workload and ensure that deadlines are realistic and achievable. With business moving at a pace, ensure that that your

workload is manageable, deadlines realistic, and objectives clear and communicated.

- Find time to relax and unwind, especially if you work in a high-pressure job. Leonardo da Vinci once wrote: "every now and then go away and have a little relaxation. To remain constantly at work will diminish your judgment. Go some distance away, so work will be in perspective and a lack of harmony is more readily seen."

- Forging relationships under pressure can be important in creating a social support group among working colleagues. Most people are working in organizations undergoing constant change, with heavier workloads and impossible deadlines but transforming pressure into a Dunkirk Spirit, into team building and camaraderie can make the journey to achieving objectives much easier and keep stress at bay.

- Be humble in your relationships with people at work. "Never think of yourself as too good for any job" is a mantra that should be practiced by senior people in management or in any other walk of life. Humility and a "down to earth" attitude to others will help to forge more meaningful relationships and a culture of trust where the pressures of work can be surfaced and dealt with quickly.

- It's always worthwhile having a passion outside work, whether in the arts, sports, education, or a specific hobby. As Vincent van Gogh once wrote "I put my heart and soul into my work, and lost my mind in the process."

- Create authentic and positive relationships with others at work. It can provide you with a "stress prevention inoculation," as many of the problems in the workplace are associated with people problems. Being yourself, treating people with respect and being supportive and kind are critical characteristics of people who cope best with the pressures of work.

- Delegate work to other people rather than keeping it to yourself. Many senior people in the workplace try to do everything themselves, but find after a period of time that they are unable to cope. Not only is delegating good for you by relieving "overload stress," but also it is "value/trust confirming" for the recipient, who can feel that you value and trust his or her expertise to manage that particular area, problem, etc.

- Be resilient at all times. There are four characteristics of resilience: confidence, purposefulness, adaptability, and social support. Confidence is about having feelings of competence and effectiveness in coping with stress situations. Purposefulness is having a clear purpose, clear values, drive, and direction. Adaptability is about being flexible and adapting to changing situations which are beyond our control. And social support is building good relationships with others and seeking support when needed to overcome adverse situations.

- Integrity and trust are keys to effective working relationships and a more open and collegiate climate at work. As long as there is a bedrock of trust, people will be able to take the risks that business requires. Fear of failure usually leads to lack of innovation and people behaving in such a way that it has significant negative consequences for the performance of the business and also encourages the staff to be less open.

- Get plenty of rest and recuperation. As John Ruskin, the social reformer, wrote in 1851, "in order that people may be happy in their work, these three things are needed: they must be fit for it, they must not do too much of it, and they must have a sense of success in it."

- Try to get away from a problem or relationship difficulty that you are having trouble dealing with and come back to it afresh.

- Get a good work/life balance and make sure you allow time for family and friends. You need to switch off from work-related problems when you get home. This is achieved by not accessing your computer or smartphone to pick up emails, and ensure that you spend quality time with your family and close friends. This also means taking exercise and doing things for people outside of work, whether charitable or in the community. This can inoculate you from the stresses of your job.

- Mentally prepare and visualize the task ahead. There is a great deal of psychology on "coping imagery," where an individual imagines or visualizes what might happen when you are doing a major presentation at work or going for an important job interview. What you need to do is run through various scenarios of a potential stressful event. Step (1) Think about the situation you are stressed about; Step (2) Note the aspects of the situation; Step (3) Develop ways to deal with it; Step (4) Visualize yourself in that situation, slowly picture yourself coping with each anticipated difficulty that arises, repeating this four or five times and Step (5) Practice this again whenever you are confronted by the same situation.

- And finally … remember, nothing is more important in life than your health, your family, and your happiness. As the US President Abraham Lincoln once wrote "It is not the years in your life which are important,
- but the life in your years."

Index

Printed and bound by CPI Group (UK) Ltd, Croydon, CR0 4YY

This book is due for return on or before the last date shown below.